Vegan Diet For Beginners

150 Delicious Recipes And Eight Weeks Of Diet Plans

By Jessica Brooks

Second Edition

Disclaimer – Please read!

The information provided in this book is designed to provide helpful information on the subjects discussed. This book is not meant to be used, nor should it be used, to diagnose or treat any medical condition. For diagnosis or treatment of any medical problem, consult your own physician. The publisher and author are not responsible for any specific health or allergy needs that may require medical supervision and are not liable for any damages or negative consequences from any treatment, action, application or preparation, to any person reading or following the information in this book. References are provided for informational purposes only and do not constitute endorsement of any websites or other sources. Readers should be aware that the websites listed in this book may change.

Table of Contents

Jessica Brooks

As a result, there has been a significant growth in diseases around the world that relate directly to animal food products. For example: fatty substances in the blood stream, called cholesterol, will build up inside of the coronary arteries and restrict blood flow to the heart, which can cause angina (severe chest pain) or heart attacks. Cholesterol is naturally produced by humans and animals. It is essential for cell walls, but when dietary cholesterol is consumed, something only existing in animal products like meat and eggs and dairy, it often stays in the blood stream. And this is what collects in the blood vessels and creates the disease. This is called Coronary artery disease and the rates of it rose in the 1960's.

Today, over 500,000 Americans go under the knife for coronary bypass surgery, to alleviate this issue by removing a healthy artery from the leg and replacing the blocked artery in the heart. These operations cost nearly $50 billion in health care costs.

In the 1960's Dr. T. Colin Campbell worked in the Philippines trying desperately to give malnourished children more protein. In an effort to reduce costs, his colleagues decided to avoid animal based proteins. Soon, he discovered that the affluent families in the area, consuming a lot of animal based foods, were the people most likely to have children highly susceptible to liver cancer. Liver cancer is something which often occurs in adults so the high rates among children were significant for many reasons. At the same time an Indian medical journal published a paper titled "The Effect of Dietary Protein on Carcinogenesis of Aflatoxin". The test administered aflatoxin to rats and fed them casein, the main protein in milk. They used 20% protein of total calories and 5% protein of total calories for their study. The results indicated that the diets of 20% casein increased cancer while 5% decreased it. Recognizing that animal protein had a direct link to higher rates of cancer, Dr. T. Colin Campbell changed the focus of his work.

Around this same time, the diet in America was changing yet again. Fast food franchises exploded and more people began using them as a method of feeding themselves and their families. At the same time, the rate of cancer-related deaths in America rose.

In 1971, Richard Nixon initiated what was called the "war on cancer" or the "Cancer Act of 1971". By 1978 Dr. Caldwell Esselstyn was chairman of the task force for breast cancer. He began researching breast cancer rates around the world. In Kenya, in 1978, the chances of a female contracting breast cancer were 82 times lower compared to the United States. Dr. Caldwell Esselstyn saw similar numbers for other cancer types. In Japan in 1958, there were only 18 autopsy proven deaths caused by prostate cancer. In the same year, the population of the U.S. was twice that of Japan, but the autopsy proven deaths by prostate cancer exceeded 14,000. In the early 1970's the risk of heart disease in rural China was at a rate 12 times lower compared to the risk of heart disease in America. In Papua New Guinea heart disease was hardly ever encountered at all! The link was animal products. In these areas with lower rates of cancer deaths, there was not access to the animal products that Americans were consuming en masse. Even more compelling is traditionally overlooked historical data; in 1939 the Germans had occupied Norway. The first thing they did was compensate animals and livestock to give their troops supplies. The Norwegians had to consume plant based foods during this time only. From 1939 until 1945 the rates of death by circulatory disease dropped dramatically. In 1938 the rate of death per 10,000 people from circulatory was around 31%. During the German occupation it plummeted to 24%. After the Germans left, meat and dairy was brought back, and the rates of strokes and heart attacks went right back up where it had been before the occupation.

The causal link between animal based foods and our current health concerns has been scientifically backed by today. In Hawaii, for example, Dr. John McDougall who, in the mid 1970's, studied those immigrant families who worked in the sugar cane fields and found that those raised in Asia before immigrating were always trim and did not have heart disease, prostate cancer, bone cancer, rheumatoid arthritis, and a myriad of other diseases. They were in their 80's and 90's and could fully function. But their children, raised on American diets, became fatter and sicker. Their children's children became even more so. The diet was the only difference. The first generation consumed rice and vegetables in their native lands while their children consumed dairy products and meats.

By 1975, Dr. Campbell investigated the work discovered in the Philippines. He conducted a study similar to the Indian study with 20% and 5% casein fed to rats. The results were the same: a greater risk of early tumor growth and cancer in those with a 20% diet. The findings were taken a step further. The test rats were kept in a single group and were switched back and forth at three week intervals between five and twenty percent proteins. The results showed that whenever the rats were on the 20% protein diet the early liver tumor growth rates exploded, but when moved back down to the 5% rates, the cancer growth went down. The overall idea was that cancer growth could be turned on or off by adjusting the intake of protein. He even discovered that a 20% diet of plant based protein did not promote cancer like animal protein. Soon Dr. Campbell found a large scale population study to confirm the previous studies.

In China in 1974, the Premier was hospitalized with bladder cancer. He opted to give his country an understanding of cancer by initiating one of the biggest and most thorough scientific studies to date. 650,000 researchers catalogued the mortality patterns of different cancers between 1973 and 1975. The study followed every part of China and over 880 million people. Dr. Campbell visited China and found the book of the cancer mortality rates in China. Published in 1981, this atlas was the result of the nationwide study. Certain types of cancers were clustered in "hot spots" in China. For example, esophageal cancer was a 400 fold difference between different Chinese counties. In the U.S. there was only a 3 fold difference at the same time. The study then focused on why this existed, since genetically the people were the same and yet had such significant differences. The result unsurprisingly, was that it related to environment and more specifically, diet.

A follow up study was conducted which the New York Times author Jane E. Brody later called the "most comprehensive large study ever undertaken of the relationship between diet and the risk of developing disease".

The project considered 367 diet and environmental variables, surveying the diet and lifestyle of 65,000 people, taking urine and blood samples across 65 counties in China, located in rural or semi-rural areas. In 1983, the data was analyzed. This process took years, but in 1990 the results were published. This identified 94,000 correlations between diet and disease. Detailed tables and charts present the raw data, cross referenced to demonstrate the reliability. The key message taken from the analysis is simple: plant food based diet, or vegan diet, is always associated with lower mortality rates from cancers, stroke, and coronary heart disease.

Their work, and work since, proves that many of our most crippling health conditions can be reduced, if not eradicated, by eating a whole food, plant based diet. Consuming foods that come from plants, and avoiding animal based foods like meat, dairy, and eggs, as well as processed foods can treat and prevent disease better than any modern prescription medications.

The Crux of the Matter

A whole food, plant based diet is one that is centered on unrefined and whole plants. It is a diet that focuses on fruits, vegetables, tubers, legumes and whole grains while excluding meat (including fish), dairy products, eggs, refined foods such as bleached flour, oil, refined sugar and anything else that is taken from animals or hurts animals in the process.

While this may seem like a striking change, it is the same way that people have survived for thousands of years. The foods are satisfying and delicious. You can use these foods to make altered versions of familiar cuisine such as lasagna, burritos, and pizza.

What is included in the diet?

Things like the following:

Fruit: bananas, oranges, cherries, mangoes, blueberries, strawberries, grapes and apples.

Vegetables: broccoli, kale, carrots, cauliflower, lettuce, collard greens, carrots and zucchini.

Tubers and starch vegetables: potatoes, winter squash, green peas, yams, yucca and corn.

Whole grains: whole wheat, quinoa, millet, rice, oats and barley.

Legumes: Lima beans, lentils, chickpeas, kidney beans, black beans and cannellini beans.

Be aware that isn't an exhaustive list by any means! I include a much more thorough list of approved foods later in the book.

One of the key things to understand here is that a vegan diet is one that is based on whole food and plants, but it is not just vegetables.

Many people think that it requires you to only eat vegetables but that is very far from the truth. Leafy vegetables are important but they offer low calorie, i.e. energy, and are therefore not sustainable over the long term. It is nearly impossible to gain enough calories from just leafy vegetables. That is why you might feel hungry after you eat, start experiencing cravings, or even binging. These are all the result of not eating enough, not of changing your diet.

That being said, vegetables are a large part of this but they are not the only thing you should have on your plate.

Many people today emphasize meat as the center of their plates. As you transition into this new diet, that starts to change. Now you will start centering your plate on starch based foods, that many people consider "comfort foods". These are so often stigmatized and yet they are the exact foods on which cultures around the world have and still continue to thrive upon. This includes tubers like sweet potatoes and potatoes, as well as starchy vegetables like peas and corn, lots of legumes like black beans and chickpeas, and whole grains such as quinoa and brown rice.

They are of course prepared a bit differently, excluding the dairy for example, but they are still delicious. You can enjoy tasty recipes that are healthy and delicious.
Instead of eating for a particular nutrient, try and change your mind frame to focus on the whole package. This will help lead you away from high animal product consumption and will help you avoid harmful substances like the dietary cholesterol found only in animal products.

No single food contains a single nutrient. Any food you eat contains countless nutrients and what matters most is that you consume the whole package. The whole food based plant diet gives you all of the nutrients you need save for vitamin B12 and the proportions are consistent with your natural human needs.

Turning to the vegan diet brings with it profound benefits for your overall well-being. That said, let's dive right in to how you can start converting your diet today!

Chapter Two: Starting Your Diet

15 helpful tips for jumping into the Vegan Diet

1. Have an open mind. Try not to focus on the stigma associated with "hippies" and "vegan" diets. Think of it more as a whole food, plant based diet. A good attitude will help you go a long way. Friends that you know will mock you perhaps don't need to know about your choice until they have personally noticed improvements in your appearance and energy. This is a tough decision and while it can seem strong to stand in the face of opposition, too much opposition will weigh you down. So stick with those who support you at first.

2. If you are cooking at home, allow additional time for the preparations. For many people, designing meals that revolve around whole foods and plants is new, and it can take a lot of extra preparation at the start. Expect to spend a bit longer cooking before you start and it will not present itself as a frustration. Be assured that as you gain experience with the new style of cooking and preparing food your speed will increase!

3. Look over your pantry. Make sure you stock it with whole grains and beans, dried rice, lentils, etc... You want to either prepare and store, or buy vegan friendly sauces and dips too. If you go to cook a vegan meal and all you see in the cupboards are meat based condiments and processed foods, it will be a challenge.

4. Start making vegan versions of meals you already love. You will hardly notice the difference, but your body certainly will. I have provided loads of examples later in the book and there is a huge amount of recipes online.

5. Read as many recipe books and recipes as you can, including all of those listed in the back of this book. The

more you know, the more excited you will be about exploring new options. You will be stunned at how many exciting versions of meals you love can be made vegan friendly!

6. Try dairy alternatives, but start with one to two alternatives per week. This will allow your body to better adjust.

7. Sample vegan foods in places that serve vegan friendly options. There are many new restaurants that focus on this type of diet, and you can locate some in your area. Most restaurants will provide vegan friendly options if you just ask.

8. Avoid convenience foods. You will not enjoy vegan frozen pizzas or frozen burger patties. Seriously, you will be much better off if you just make them at home. The extra work is well worth it. If you hesitate at all, think back to the last time you ate a delicious frozen meal. It probably never happened. Now increase the bad taste and sick feeling you had all night after by a factor of five and that is what your frozen vegan foods will be.

9. Stick to the produce section. You will find that you can load up now on vegetables that you may never have tried before. If you see something in the produce area that you have never even heard of, buy it and look up some recipes for it. See how you like it. You might be surprised! Try everything once, you never know when you are going to find your new favorite food. And remember, that in most stores, the layout for healthy eating is to stick to the perimeter where the produce is. Things in the middle are frozen foods and processed foods. Avoid those.

10. Do not try and "explain" yourself to others. Stick to your guns and let their question serve as a starting point for a serious conversation about how you agree with the science today, or you have always wanted to try it and you will get more respect from the person on the other end. You might even influence their thinking!

11. When you are heading on a road trip or going to the office, pack your own food. You will feel so much better if you have a bag of carrot sticks and red pepper slices with a package of homemade hummus for your snack or a good salad. Make your own trail mix and see how much easier it will be should you wind up in an unfamiliar location and starving. And on that note...

12. If you *are* in an unfamiliar location and you absolutely need food, do not starve yourself just because you cannot find a vegan option. The moment your eating habits stop being fun, they will seem more like a fad diet and you won't want to continue. Just look for the healthiest option you can find and move on.

13. If you slip up here or there, don't worry. Everyone does. And just because you accidentally had fish sauce or ate something prepared with egg does not mean you are a failure or that you are responsible for the harm and death of millions of animals. No one will kick you out of their group or stop interacting with you because of it. This is a lifestyle change and that takes time.

14. Stay strong! This type of change can be really difficult at first. You might struggle to find vegan friendly foods at home or out and you might think that it is just easier to cave. But don't give in, the health benefits are so worth it!

15. Finally, don't judge other people just because you disagree with their eating habits. If you don't want to be judged by them, don't judge back.

Shopping Guide

When you shop as a vegan you should make sure that you fill your pantry first with the dry staple foods. This includes the following:

- Dried or canned lentils, chickpeas, kidney beans, and pinto beans
- Whole grain pasta and noodles
- Silken tofu
- Unsweetened coconut milk or coconut milk
- Canned tomato and vegetable products
- Soy sauce, vegan mustard, chutney, and other condiments
- Dried fruits
- Thickeners
- Egg replacement powder
- Vegetable broth
- Vinegars
- Grains such as millet, barley, rolled oats, couscous, rice
- Whole grain flour
- Whole grain bread and tortillas
- Nuts and seeds
- Oils
- Almond butter
- Lemons and limes
- Fresh ginger
- Garlic

Then you need to buy your produce. This is really based on whatever you decide to cook, and whatever items you need. With produce you will have to make more regular trips to get fresh products, as not all of them will save well. But that is well worth the health benefits you will receive.

Growing At Home

One of the easiest ways to transition into this diet is to start a small garden at home, even if you just have a standing greenhouse on a balcony or on a window sill. Growing a garden at home can save you so much time and money over the long run and will make it easier to maintain this healthier diet. Instead of having to hope that you can find the ingredients you need, free from any chemicals or additives, you can rest assured knowing that they are right there in your garden. You can stick to a whole food, plant based diet and enjoy the multiple benefits that are associated with tending a small garden. All you'll need to do is stock up on whole grains and then pick daily from your garden the items you want to include for your meals.

A full guide to growing foods at home would warrant another full book so I will simply highlight some of the best foods to grow at home and encourage you to do a little research! It's truly worth it, one of my favorite parts of the day is picking from my home mini-farm and consuming the foods right away, as fresh as can be.

Here is a list of the ten fruits, vegetables and herbs that I believe are the easiest to grow at home: Sweetcorn, peppers, tomatoes, zucchini, cilantro, basil and mint, all kinds of berries, kale and peas.

Eating Out

As a vegan, eating out can be difficult. If you know you are taking a trip soon, you can use resources such as PETA's website or the Happy Cow website to find vegetarian and vegan restaurant chains near your location. Of course, your office might be sending you to a place where fried mayonnaise balls are the norm, in which case, you might want to pack your own food or find accommodations with a small kitchenette and prepare food yourself.

If you are invited to dinner somewhere, plan ahead by looking up the menu. You may not be able to find vegan friendly items, but you might be able to find a vegetarian option. Alternatively, ask if you can modify your foods ahead of time, such as removing chicken from a chicken stir fry. Do not be afraid to call the restaurant if there is no website or menu posted and ask them ahead of time if they can accommodate vegan diets. If you let them know ahead of time, they might be able to speak with the chef before you and your group arrives. You can even ask if they have a vegetarian menu. Some higher end restaurants have a secret vegetarian menu that they only pull out upon request. You might have to lend a hand to the chef by asking them to make a vegetarian dish a vegan one through replacing butter with oil or removing the cheese. If nothing else, you can ask them for a handful of side dishes, like steamed broccoli, beans, and rice, and use that to create your full meal.

If you will be severely limited when going out, say your friends are taking you to a Brazilian restaurant where the dinner is meat with sides of endless meat; you can eat before you go so that you don't need much when you go out. Alternatively, you can search for ethnic restaurants, as these are most likely to have easily modified vegetarian options.

The key here is planning ahead!

Making Small Changes

One of the best ways to remain healthy mentally, physically, and emotionally is changing your diet. Do not rapidly change your diet because this can cause diarrhea, gas, or abdominal cramps. However, gradual changes and higher incorporations of fiber can help your system reduce the bacteria in your colon. There are certain foods which can be integrated into your diet to help increase fiber intake and reduce problems within your colon and digestive system. Whole grains, fruits, and vegetables high in fiber can help to offset these drastic changes to your body.

Cravings

As you make the change toward the vegan diet, your body might start to crave things. When you start to make dietary changes, you may need to test the waters a bit with different recipes and you might have to experience a learning curve before you can find meals and recipes that give you all of the nutrients you need and help to keep you energized. You may experience cravings at first which indicate that your body is not consuming enough. But you might also get a craving for another reason.

Your body will naturally crave things when it requires a particular nutrient and being able to recognize those cravings can enable you to incorporate whatever nutrient is missing into your next meal.

When you feel a deep crave for chocolate it means your body needs magnesium. When this happens try to incorporate the following into your next meal:

- Nuts
- Seeds

- Fruit
- Legumes

If your body is craving sweets or sugary foods it needs things such as Chromium, Phosphorous, Sulphur, Carbon, or Tryptophan. When this happens it is best to incorporate:

- Fresh fruit
- Broccoli
- Raisins
- Sweet potatoes
- Grapes
- Spinach
- Nuts

When you feel a deep crave for bread or pasta your body needs nitrogen. When this happens try to incorporate the following into your next meal:

- Beans
- Nuts

When you feel a deep crave for oily foods or fatty foods your body needs calcium. When this happens try to incorporate the following into your next meal

- Green leafy vegetables
- Broccoli

If you are overeating your body may need silicon or tyrosine so you should eat:

- Spinach
- Nuts
- Seeds
- Fruit
- Vegetables
- Raisins

Chapter Three: Diet Plans

Creating a Diet Plan

When you make the switch to the strict diet, your goal is to consume high nutrient, non-toxic foods.

The 10 Super food groups to include in your vegan diet

Leafy Greens:

Leafy greens include kale, chard, and spinach. You may prefer kale because it is high in flavonoids, carotenoids, antioxidants, Omega 3, fiber, vitamin K, calcium, folate, and iron. Spinach has twice the fiber as other greens and gives you folate, vitamin B1, B2, and B6, vitamin A, calcium, vitamin C, Omega 3, iron, niacin, phosphorus, beta-carotenes, and will reduce your blood pressure and help fight against heart disease and bone degeneration.

Berries:

Some of the most beneficial berries include; strawberries, raspberries, blueberries and goji berries. Berries have fructose in them, but your body needs this sugar in order to stay healthy. Blueberries have antioxidants, vitamins A, C, E, and K, fiber, zinc, calcium, manganese, lycopene, niacin, and will fight heart disease.

Quinoa:

Although it's usually referred to as a grain, it is actually a seed related to spinach and beets. It comes in a variety of colors and has two great selling points: it's gluten-free and it's a great, complete source of protein. Complete sources of protein are rare in the plant world, making quinoa an excellent source for vegans. It is high in iron and calcium as well as being a great source of manganese, magnesium, copper and fiber. It is really easy to cook, and also works great in a salad.

Amaranth:

Another gluten-free grain that is a great source of protein, folate and vitamin B6. It is a good source of fiber and is one of the few grains to contain the amino acid lysine. It is second only to quinoa in terms of iron content and it has been shown to reduce cholesterol levels. It is also one of the only grains to be a source of vitamin C!

Sweet potatoes:

These tubers are a wonderful source of vitamins and minerals. Rich in Vitamins A, C, D and B6 and full of minerals; potassium, iron and magnesium these potatoes will be a staple of your diet.

Kiwi:

These delicious, slightly sour fruits are proof that great things can come in small packages. One large kiwi can provide your entire recommended daily dosage of vitamin C by itself! They are full of vitamins A and E, vitamin E being a vitamin that vegans can sometimes become deficient in. I recommend that you eat at least a few of these a week.

Flax and Chia seeds:

These seeds are one the greatest sources of Omega-3 and 6 for a vegan. The other common option for consuming these fatty acids is fish oils, clearly not an option for us! Chia seeds are a good protein source as well as being full of calcium, potassium, fiber and vitamin B complex. Whilst flax seeds have been suggested to help fight cancer by inhibiting tumor growth and by reducing hormone metabolism.

Avocadoes:

As discussed earlier, the saturated fats of animals clog people's arteries. However the fats found in plant foods are good for our health. Avocadoes are a wonderful source of monosaturated fats, whilst also being full of potassium, folate and vitamins K and E. They are a lovely addition to most sandwiches or salads.

Spirulina and Chlorella:

Spirulina is a cyanobacteria that is now considered one of the most nutritious food sources on the planet! The United Nations World Food Conference called it "the best food for the future". It is a complete protein source rich in B vitamins and has been reported to help correct anemia and reduce radioactive damage and lower cholesterol. Chlorella is a similar green algae that acts as a detoxifier for the body. When combined these two algae's can have a profound effect on your health. Just beware of the taste, it can take some getting used to!

Almonds:

These nuts are crammed full of vitamins, healthy fats and fiber. Due to their high fat content they are very calorie dense, making them a perfect food for snacking on. They can also be used in oatmeal, desserts and salads. Be sure to carry a small bag of these with you wherever you go!

2 x 4-Week Meal Plans

Here are two, month long diet plans for you to try out should you need a little guidance. These don't need to be followed religiously, be sure to experiment and change things around. Most of the meals listed in the diet plan are recipes provided in the later chapters. A few of the meals do not have a specific recipe, for example "Big salad using Romaine lettuce", in this case I will leave it up to you to knock up a quick meal! Be sure to choose two snacks from the snack recipe chapter each day to consume when you are feeling peckish or are in need of an energy boost!

Meal Plan 1

Week 1

Monday

Breakfast: Potatoes scramble with hot chili sauce
Lunch: Big salad using Romaine lettuce
Dinner: Black bean taquitos

Tuesday

Breakfast: Fresh strawberry and banana smoothie
Lunch: Avocado Salsa Salad
Dinner: Spinach potato tacos

Wednesday

Breakfast: Banana blueberry bars
Lunch: Sweet Potato Avocado Wraps
Dinner: Hummus filled potatoes with spinach and romaine lettuce

Thursday

Breakfast: Garlic hash browns with kale
Lunch: Chickpea avocado salad
Dinner: Stuffed Avocados

Friday

Breakfast: Green smoothie with kale and kiwi
Lunch: Salad with black beans and tomatoes
Dinner: Stuffed Peppers

Saturday

Breakfast: Pumpkin Muffins
Lunch: Stuffed Portobello Mushrooms
Dinner: Vegetable stew

Sunday

Breakfast: Coconut pancakes with blueberries or with strawberries
Lunch: Steamed vegetables and brown rice
Dinner: Corn and black bean cakes

Week 2

Monday

Breakfast: Pumpkin Muffins
Lunch: Avocado Salsa Salad
Dinner: Corn and black bean cakes

Tuesday

Breakfast: Green smoothie with spinach and peaches
Lunch: Chickpea avocado salad
Dinner: Hummus filled potatoes with grilled asparagus and caramelized onions

Wednesday

Breakfast: Homemade Almond Milk Oatmeal
Lunch: Salad with black beans and tomatoes
Dinner: Vegetable stew

Thursday

Breakfast: Potatoes scramble with hot chili sauce
Lunch: Stuffed Portobello Mushrooms
Dinner: Hummus filled potatoes

Friday

Breakfast: Banana blueberry bars
Lunch: Sweet Potato Avocado Wraps
Dinner: Spinach potato tacos

Saturday

Breakfast: Potatoes scramble with hot chili sauce
Lunch: Chickpea and Broccoli Salad
Dinner: Spinach potato tacos

Sunday

Breakfast: Coconut pancakes with strawberries
Lunch: Salad with romaine lettuce
Dinner: Corn and black bean cakes

Meal Plan #2

Week 1

Monday

Breakfast: Pumpkin pie squares
Lunch: Tortilla soup
Dinner: Corn and black bean cakes

Tuesday

Breakfast: Chocolate pumpkin loaf
Lunch: Coconut curry vegetable stir fry
Dinner: Spinach potato tacos

Wednesday

Breakfast: Garlic hash browns with kale
Lunch: Asian lettuce wrap with pineapple
Dinner: Black bean and corn patties with spinach and romaine
lettuce

Thursday

Breakfast: Pumpkin pie squares
Lunch: Sweet Potato Avocado Wraps
Dinner: Stuffed Peppers

Friday

Breakfast: Banana and pear green smoothie
Lunch: Salad with black beans and tomatoes
Dinner: Creamy tomato soup with almond bread

Saturday

Breakfast: Pumpkin Muffins
Lunch: Chickpea and Broccoli Salad
Dinner: Black bean taquitos

Sunday

Breakfast: Coconut pancakes with strawberries
Lunch: Avocado Salsa Salad
Dinner: Vegetable stew

Week 2

Monday

Breakfast: Pumpkin pie squares
Lunch: Stuffed Portobello Mushrooms
Dinner: Stuffed Peppers

Tuesday

Breakfast: Assorted sautéed vegetables including spinach and broccoli
Lunch: Tortilla soup
Dinner: Spinach potato tacos

Wednesday

Breakfast: Pumpkin Muffins
Lunch: Black bean patty with asparagus
Dinner: Asian lettuce wrap with pineapple

Thursday

Breakfast: Banana blueberry bars
Lunch: Coconut curry stir fry
Dinner: Vegetable stew

Friday

Breakfast: Green smoothie with kale and kiwi
Lunch: Chickpea and Broccoli Salad
Dinner: Italian white bean soup

Saturday

Breakfast: Potato pancakes
Lunch: Salad with black beans and tomatoes
Dinner: Black bean taquitos

Sunday

Breakfast: Garlic hash browns with kale
Lunch: Tasty Bean Burgers
Dinner: Vegetarian Sheppard's Pie

Week 3

Monday

Breakfast: Banana blueberry bars
Lunch: Chickpea and Broccoli Salad
Dinner: Stuffed Peppers

Tuesday

Breakfast: Green smoothie with kale and kiwi
Lunch: Avocado Salsa Salad
Dinner: Hummus filled potatoes

Wednesday

Breakfast: Mixed nuts and berries
Lunch: Tortilla soup
Dinner: Italian white bean soup

Thursday

Breakfast: Pink smoothie
Lunch: Salad with black beans and tomatoes
Dinner: Pumpkin chili

Friday

Breakfast: Coconut pancakes with real cinnamon
Lunch: Tasty Bean Burgers
Dinner: Spinach potato tacos

Saturday

Breakfast: Chocolate pumpkin loaf
Lunch: Zucchini with sweet potatoes
Dinner: Vegetable stew

Sunday

Breakfast: Potato pancakes
Lunch: Sweet Potato Avocado Wraps
Dinner: Black bean taquitos

Week 4

Monday

Breakfast: Fruit Salad with Cinnamon
Lunch: Salad with roasted chickpeas and tomatoes
Dinner: Hummus filled potatoes

Tuesday

Breakfast: Assorted sautéed vegetables including spinach and broccoli
Lunch: Salad with black beans and tomatoes
Dinner: Caramelized vegetables with butternut squash

Wednesday

Breakfast: Chocolate pumpkin loaf
Lunch: Sweet Potato Avocado Wraps
Dinner: Stuffed Peppers

Thursday

Breakfast: Banana and pear green smoothie
Lunch: Tortilla soup
Dinner: Black bean taquitos

Friday

Breakfast: Fruit Salad with Cinnamon
Lunch: Avocado Salsa Salad
Dinner: Black beans and wild rice with steamed vegetables

Saturday

Breakfast: Coconut pancakes with blueberries
Lunch: Chickpea and Broccoli Salad
Dinner: Italian white bean soup

Sunday

Breakfast: Potatoes scramble with hot chili sauce
Lunch: Tasty Bean Burgers
Dinner: Hummus filled potatoes

Jessica Brooks

Chapter Four: 60 Breakfast Recipes

Below you will find ten recipes that you can use for your breakfasts. Make sure you try different whole food items and spices to find a flavor that best suits your taste!

Potatoes scramble with hot chili sauce

Ingredients:

- 1 ½ cup chopped red onion
- 3 tablespoons yellow mustard
- ½ teaspoon ground allspice
- 1 ½ teaspoon chopped jalapeno
- 1 cup water
- 2 pounds potatoes
- 5 finely chopped tomatoes
- ½ cup cilantro
- 3 tablespoons lime juice
- Whole grain tortillas or whole grain bread

Instructions:

- In a large skillet combine 1 1/2 cups of chopped red onion, three Tablespoons of yellow mustard, 1/4 teaspoon ground allspice, 1 1/2 teaspoons of chopped jalapeno, and one cup of water. Combine these and bring it to simmer. Cover the pot and cook until your onions are translucent. Then add 2 pounds of potatoes cut into cubes and cook for five minutes on high heat. Reduce the heat to medium and cover it, allowing the potatoes to cook until they are tender. You can prepare this dish up to two days ahead of time and leave it in your refrigerator in an airtight container until you are ready to serve it. When you are ready to serve reheat it if necessary.

- Just before you serve, stir into five finely chopped tomatoes, 1/2 cup of freshly chopped cilantro, and 3 tablespoons of fresh lime juice taken from one or two limes. You can wrap this scramble in warm whole-grain tortillas or you can toast six slices of whole grain bread and distribute the scramble on top.

Potato pancakes

Ingredients:

- two large potatoes
- one large zucchini
- 1/2 cup of yellow onion
- 1/2 cup of oat flour
- 1 teaspoon of baking powder
- 1/2 teaspoon of black pepper

Instructions:

- Preheat your oven to 425° and cover two baking sheets with parchment paper.
- Finely grate large potatoes, one large zucchini, and 1/2 cup of yellow onion. Spread half of your grated vegetable mixture onto a kitchen towel and ring out excess moisture.
- Combine 1/2 cup of oat flour, 1 teaspoon of baking powder and 1/2 teaspoon of black pepper. Add your vegetables and use your hands to evenly cover the vegetable mixture with your flour and baking powder mixture.
- Then scoop 1/4 cup of the potato mixture and tighten it into a ball. Flatten the ball with the palm of your hand so that it forms a pancake shape. Place it onto your prepared pan with about 2 inches in between each pancake.
- Bake this for 12 minutes. Flip the pancakes over and bake for another 12 minutes until you have achieved your desired level of crispy feeling. Cover with your favorite condiment.

Chocolate pumpkin loaf

Ingredients:

- 1/4 cup of unsweetened applesauce
- 1/3 cup of unsweetened cocoa powder
- 1 1/2 cups of whole flour
- 1/2 teaspoon of ground cinnamon
- 1/4 teaspoon of ground nutmeg
- 1/4 teaspoon of ground ginger
- 1/8 teaspoon of ground cloves
- 3/4 teaspoon of salt
- 3/4 teaspoon of baking soda.
- one third of a cup of boiling water
- 1 cup of puréed pumpkin
- 1 cup of dry sweetener
- 3 tablespoons of almond butter
- 1 teaspoon of pure vanilla
- 1/2 cup of grain sweetened chocolate chips

Instructions:

- Preheat your oven to 350°. Have an 8" x 4" nonstick baking pan ready. Bring some water; it does not matter how much, to boil in a tea kettle. Combine 1/4 cup of unsweetened applesauce with 1/3 cup of unsweetened cocoa powder. Sift together 1 1/2 cups of whole flour, 1/2 teaspoon of ground cinnamon, 1/4 teaspoon of ground nutmeg, 1/4 teaspoon of ground ginger, and 1/8 teaspoon of ground cloves. Mix this together with 3/4 teaspoon of salt and 3/4 teaspoon of baking soda.
- Measure one third of a cup of your boiling water and pour into your bowl with the mixture. This will create a chocolate sauce. Then add 1 cup of puréed pumpkin, 1 cup of dry sweetener, 3 tablespoons of almond butter and 1 teaspoon of pure vanilla. Mix all of this together.
- Dump half of your flour mix into the chocolate mix and stir gently then add 1 tablespoon of boiling water and

stir again. Add the remainder of your flour mix and a 2nd tablespoon of boiling water. Stir this until it is smooth but be careful not to over mix it. Then fold in 1/2 cup of grain sweetened chocolate chips. Smooth your batter into your loaf pan and bake it for 60 minutes. Remove the loaf from the oven and allow it to cool for 10 minutes before serving.

Homemade Almond Milk Oatmeal

Ingredients:

- 250g almonds
- 1 litre of water
- 2 pitted dates
- 1 tablespoon of vanilla extract
- One cup oats
- ½ teaspoon of cinnamon

Instructions:

- To make the almond milk:
  - Mix 250g almonds
  - 1 liter of water
  - 2 pitted dates
  - 1 tablespoon of vanilla extract
- To make the oatmeal:
  - Bring mix oats to boil in almond milk and top with ½ teaspoon of cinnamon

Place all ingredients in a blender and blend for thirty seconds until creamy. Strain with muslin and store in the refrigerator.

Banana blueberry bars

Ingredients:

- one cup of dates
- 1 1/2 cup of apple juice
- 2 cups of rolled oats
- 3/4 teaspoon of ground cinnamon
- 1/4 teaspoon ground nutmeg.
- one cup of rolled oats
- three ripe bananas
- 1 teaspoon of vanilla
- 1/2 cup of walnuts
- one cup of fresh blueberries

Instructions:

- In a small bowl soak one cup of dates in 1 1/2 cups of apple juice for 10 minutes.
- Preheat your oven to 375°. Line a 9" x 9" baking pan with parchment paper and cut slits in the corners of your paper so that it lies flat.
- In a medium-size bowl combine 2 cups of rolled oats with 3/4 teaspoon of ground cinnamon and 1/4 teaspoon ground nutmeg. Set that aside.
- Place one cup of rolled oats with three ripe bananas and 1 teaspoon of vanilla extract into a blender. Add the dates strained to the blender and blend until smooth.
- Pour this mixture into the dry ingredients and mix well. Stir in 1/2 cup of walnuts and one cup of blueberries.
- Pour the batter into your baking pan and cook for 30 minutes. Allow to cool for 10 minutes before serving.

Garlic hash browns with kale

Ingredients:

- two large potatoes
- salt and pepper to taste
- six minced garlic cloves
- 1 cup shredded kale

Instructions:

- Preheat oven to 375°.
- Shred two large potatoes and pack them dry. Add salt and pepper to taste. Spread them on a baking sheet and bake them for 10 minutes. Remove them from the oven and toss them with six minced garlic cloves and then pop them back onto your baking sheet. Cook them for another five minutes.
- While these are baking sauté your shredded kale over medium heat with 1/8 inch of water and salt. Do not replenish your water as it starts to evaporate. Once your kale is soft, set it aside and allow it to cool. Season your shredded potatoes to your liking and top with your kale. You can even cover this delicious meal with your favorite salsa or dipping sauce.

Pumpkin Muffins

Ingredients:

- 1 and ½ cup of almond flour
- ¾ cup of canned pumpkins
- 3 large egg substitutes
- 1 teaspoon of baking powder
- 1 teaspoon of baking soda
- ½ teaspoon of ground cinnamon
- 1 and ½ teaspoon of pumpkin pie spice
- 1/8 teaspoon of sea salt
- ¼ cup of agave nectar
- 2 teaspoons of almond butter

Instructions:

- Preheat your oven to 350 degrees.
- Coat your muffin pan with coconut oil.
- Add:
    - 1 and ½ cup of almond flour
    - ¾ cup of canned pumpkins
    - 3 large egg substitutes
    - 1 teaspoon of baking powder
    - 1 teaspoon of baking soda
    - ½ teaspoon of ground cinnamon
    - 1 and ½ teaspoon of pumpkin pie spice
    - 1/8 teaspoon of sea salt
    - ¼ cup of agave nectar
    - 2 teaspoons of almond butter

Mix them together and pour into the muffin tin evenly. Bake for 25 minutes. Sprinkle almonds on top once finished.

Coconut Pancakes

Ingredients:

- 3 egg substitutes
- ¼ cup of coconut flour
- ½ teaspoon of baking powder
- ½ teaspoon of organic maple syrup
- Salt
- Berries of your choice

Instructions:

- Whisk 3 egg substitutes in a bowl.
- Add ¼ cup of coconut flour.
- Add ½ teaspoon of baking powder.
- Add ½ teaspoon of organic maple syrup.
- Add a pinch of salt.
- Mix well.
- Then mash berries into a bowl with one teaspoon of hot water.
- Heat coconut oil on a pan and cook pancake batter.

Scoop a helping of mashed berries on top and enjoy.

Pumpkin pie squares

Ingredients:

- 10 dates that have been pitted and diced
- 3/4 cup of water
- 1 1/2 cups of oat flour
- 2 teaspoons of pumpkin pie spice
- 1 teaspoon of vanilla extract
- 1/2 cup of unsweetened plant milk

Instructions:

- Soak 10 dates that have been pitted and diced in a bowl with 3/4 cup of water for 20 minutes. Preheat your oven to 375°.
- Place 1 1/2 cups of oat flour and 2 teaspoons of pumpkin pie spice in a large bowl place your soaked dates and the water into the bowl with 1 teaspoon of vanilla extract and 1/2 cup of unsweetened plant milk. Blend this until it is smooth. Pour the mixture into a bowl and mix with a wooden spoon until everything is smooth. Scrape your batter into in 8" x 8" baking sheet and cook for 25 minutes or until the top is lightly browned. Let the food cool for 10 minutes before you cut and serve.

Fruit Salad with Cinnamon

Ingredients:

- 1 orange
- one diced apple
- ½ cup of walnuts or pecans
- ½ teaspoon of cinnamon

Instructions:

- Add 1 peeled and diced orange to a bowl.
- Add one diced apple.
- Add ½ cup of walnuts or pecans.
- Add ½ teaspoon of cinnamon.

Mix in the bowl and sprinkle with cinnamon.

Rhubarb Porridge

Ingredients:

- ½ cup of orange juice
- 1 ½ cups of almond milk
- 1 cup of rolled oat
- 1 cup of fresh rhubarb, cut into ¼ to 1/2 inch pieces
- 3 tablespoons of brown sugar
- ½ teaspoon of ground cinnamon
- Pinch of salt
- Extra: a few tablespoons of chopped nuts

Instructions:

- In a medium saucepan combine the almond milk, juice, oats, rhubarb cinnamon and salt to taste.
- Bring the pan to boil at a medium temperature.
- Stir frequently whilst reducing the temperature until the oats and rhubarb are soft. This should take no more than 5 minutes.
- Cover the saucepan and let it stand for 5 minutes.
- Stir in the sugar.
- Top with nuts if desired.

Sunshine Smoothie

Ingredients:

- 2 cups of fresh or frozen peach slices
- 1 cup of freshly squeezed orange juice
- 1 small carrot
- 2 tablespoons of ground flaxseed
- 1 tablespoon of chopped fresh ginger

Instructions:

- Combine the ingredients in your blender and blend until smooth.
- Serve right away

Cashew Curry Oatmeal

Ingredients:

- ½ cup of rolled oats
- 3 tablespoons of golden raisins
- 1 cup of water
- 2 tablespoons of toasted chopped cashew nuts
- ¼ teaspoon of curry powder
- Pinch of salt to taste

Instructions:

- Add the water and salt to a medium saucepan and bring it to a boil.
- Stir the oats in.
- Reduce the heat to medium and cook whilst stirring regularly.
- Cook until most of the liquid has been absorbed, this should take 5 minutes.
- Remove from heat and let it stand, covered for 3 minutes.
- Sprinkle the raisins, cashews and curry powder on top.

Chai-Spiced Coconut Oatmeal

Ingredients:

- ½ cup of old-fashioned rolled oats
- 1 cup of water
- 3 tablespoons of unsweetened coconut milk
- 2 teaspoons of brown sugar
- 2 tablespoons of toasted unsweetened coconut chips
- ¼ teaspoon ground cinnamon
- 1/8 teaspoon ground ginger
- Pinch of ground black pepper
- Pinch of ground cardamom
- Pinch of salt

Instructions:

- Add water and salt to a small saucepan and bring it to a boil.
- Stir in the oats and reduce the heat to medium and cook for about 5 minutes.
- Make sure most of the liquid has been absorbed.
- Remove from the heat and let it stand, covered for 3 minutes.
- Top with coconut milk, coconut chips, brown sugar, cinnamon, ginger, cardamom and black pepper.

Sour Avocado Smoothie

Ingredients:

- 1 avocado, peeled and pitted
- ¾ cup of freshly squeezed raspberry juice
- 1 cup of freshly squeezed orange juice
- ½ cup of frozen raspberries

Instructions:

- Place all the ingredients in a blender and blend until smooth.
- Serve immediately

Nutty Maple Granola

Ingredients:

- 5 cups of old fashioned rolled oats
- 1 cup of unsweetened coconut chips
- ½ cup of water
- ½ cup of raisins
- ½ cup of dried cranberries
- ½ cup of pure maple syrup
- ½ cup of sliced almonds
- 1/3 cup of chopped pecans
- ½ cup of light brown sugar
- 1/3 cup of pumpkin seeds
- 1/3 cup of sunflower seeds
- ¼ cup of canola oil

Instructions:

- Preheat your over to 275F
- In a large bowl, mix the oats, coconut, almonds, pecans, brown sugar, pumpkin and sunflower seeds.
- In a separate bowl combine the syrup, water and oil and then pour over the oat mixture.
- Stir the mixture until well mixed.
- Spread the mixture onto a large rimmed baking sheet and bake for 45 minutes.
- Take it out of the oven and give it a stir and then continue to bake for a further 45 minutes.
- It should be golden brown and beginning to get crispy
- Stir in the cranberries and raisins and allow to cool before serving or storing.

Energy Juice

Ingredients:

- 1 medium tomato, cut into wedges
- 1 medium orange, peeled and quartered
- 1 medium green apple, cored and cut into quarters
- 3 large peeled carrots
- If desired, ice cubes

Instructions:

- In this order; tomato, apple, orange and carrots, process through your juicer.
- Fill a glass with ice and then pour the juice into the glasses to enjoy extra fresh.

Yankee Grits

Ingredients:

- 1 cup of water
- 2 teaspoons of pure maple syrup
- ¼ cup of quick-cooking grits
- 2 tablespoons of assorted dried fruit
- Salt to taste

Instructions:

- In a small saucepan bring the water, syrup and a pinch of salt to boil over a high temperature.
- Whisk in the grits and reduce the temperature to low.
- Cover and cook, stirring every minute.
- After 4 minutes the mixture should have thickened.
- Allow the mixture to cool down and then sprinkle with dried fruit before serving.

Jessica's Granola

Ingredients:

- 6 cups of old fashioned rolled oats
- 1 cup of chopped walnuts
- 1 cup of chopped almonds
- ½ a cup of maple syrup
- ¼ cup of agave nectar
- 6 tablespoons of canola oil
- 1 teaspoon of ground cinnamon
- 1 teaspoon of vanilla extract

Instructions:

- Preheat your over to 325F
- Line a large baking sheet with parchment paper
- In a large bowl, combine the oats, almonds and walnuts.
- In a medium bowl whisk the maple syrup, canola oil, agave nectar, cinnamon, vanilla and salt until blended.
- Pour the second mixture over the oats and toss.
- Spread the mixture out in the baking sheet.
- Whilst stirring every 15 minutes, bake the mixture for an hour.
- It should be lightly and evenly browned.
- Stand for at least 20 minutes before serving.

Tangy Grapefruit Compote

Ingredients:

- 1 ¾ cups of fresh cranberries
- 1 ¼ cups water
- 2, ¾ by 2 ½ inch strips of orange zest
- ½ cup of freshly squeezed orange juice
- ½ cup sugar
- 1 cinnamon stick
- 3 large red grapefruit
- Some fresh mint springs, to garnish

Instructions:

- In a medium saucepan, combine the cranberries, water, orange zest strips, orange juice, sugar and cinnamon stick.
- Bring the pain to boil of a medium-high temperature.
- For 5 minutes, cook the mixture whilst stirring often until the cranberries begin to pop.
- Transfer the mixture to a large bowl, cover and refrigerate until completely chilled.
- Prepare the grapefruit and hour before serving.
- Remove the skin with a sharp knife. Remove the white pith as well.
- Working over a bowl, cut the segments from their surrounding membranes.
- Squeeze the juice from the membranes into the bowl before discarding.
- Add the segments and the juice to the cranberry mixture.
- To serve, divide the compote amongst dessert bowls and garnish with mint

Easy Morning Smoothie

Ingredients:

- 1 cup of mixed, frozen berries
- 1 banana
- 1 small green apple
- ¼ cup of silken tofu

Instructions:

- Combine all the ingredients into a blender and blend until smooth.
- Serve immediately

Jessica Brooks

Dried Fruit Compote with Green Tea and Lemon

Ingredients:

- 3 green tea bags
- 3 cups of boiling water
- 2 tablespoons of sugar
- 2 teaspoons of freshly grated lemon zest
- 3 cups of mixed dried fruit

Instructions:

- Steep the green tea bags in boiling water for 4 minutes.
- Remove the tea bags and stir the sugar and lemon zest into the tea.
- Make sure the dried fruit are in suitable small chunks.
- Place the fruit and the tea in a slow cooker.
- Cover and cook until the fruit is plump and the liquid is syrupy.
- This should take around 4 hours on a low temperature.
- Transfer to a bowl and let it cool.
- Cover and refrigerate until cooled before serving.

Dark Green Smoothie

Ingredients:

- 2 ripe bananas
- 1 ripe conference pear, peeled and chopped
- 2 cups of chopped kale leaves
- ½ cup of freshly squeezed orange juice
- ½ cup of chilled water
- 1 tablespoon of ground flaxseed
- Ice

Instructions:

- Place all of the ingredients into a blender and blend until smooth.
- Serve immediately.

Green Tea Smoothie

Ingredients:

- 3 cups of frozen green grapes
- 2 cups of baby spinach
- 2 cups of strongly brewed green tea
- 1 medium avocado
- 2 teaspoons of agave nectar

Instructions:

- Combine all of the ingredients into a blender and blend until smooth.
- Serve immediately.

Wake-up! Energizer Smoothie

Ingredients:

- 1 ½ cups of freshly squeezed orange juice
- 1 banana
- 1 ½ cups of mixed, frozen berries
- ½ cup of silken tofu
- 1 tablespoon of sugar

Instructions:

- Combine all of the ingredients in a blender and blend until smooth.
- Serve immediately.

Jessica Brooks

Tropical Tofu Smoothie

Ingredients:

- 2 cups of diced, frozen mango
- 2 cups of fresh pineapple juice
- 1 cup of silken tofu
- ¼ cup of fresh lime juice
- 1 teaspoon of freshly grated lemon zest

Instructions:

- Combine all of the ingredients in a blender and blend until smooth.
- Serve immediately.

Chickpea Pancake

Ingredients:

- 1 green onion, finely chopped
- ½ cup of chickpea flour
- ¼ cup of red pepper, finely chopped
- ¼ teaspoon of garlic powder
- ¼ teaspoon of fine sea salt
- ¼ teaspoon of baking powder
- 1/8 teaspoon of freshly ground black pepper
- Pinch of red pepper flakes
- ½ cup + 2 tablespoons of water

Instructions:

- Prepare the vegetables and set aside.
- Preheat a 10-inch skillet over a medium temperature.
- In a small bowl, whisk together the chickpea flour, garlic powder, salt, pepper, baking powder and the red pepper flakes.
- Add the water to the mixture and whisk until there are no clumps.
- Stir the chopped vegetable in.
- When the skillet is heated, spray it generously with a non-stick cooking spray.
- Pour on all of the batter and quickly spread it out over the pan.
- Cook for 5 minutes on one side, until you can easily slide a spatula under the pancake, and it is firm enough to stay together when flipping.

- Flip the pancake and cook for another 5 minutes on this side, until lightly golden.
- Serve on a large plate and top with your favorite toppings!

Blueberry Oatmeal Waffles

Ingredients:

- 1 cup of whole-wheat flour
- 1 tablespoon of baking powder
- ½ teaspoon of salt
- ¼ teaspoon of ground allspice
- 1 cup of quick cooking oats
- 1/3 cup of unsweetened applesauce
- 1 ½ cups of almond milk
- 3 tablespoons of maple syrup
- 2 tablespoons of canola oil
- 1 teaspoon of vanilla extract
- 1 ½ cups of frozen blueberries

Instructions:

- Sift the flour, baking powder, ground allspice and salt into a mixing bowl.
- Mix in the oats.
- Make a well in the center and add the milk, applesauce, maple syrup, canola oil and vanilla extract.
- Stir until well mixed.
- Let the batter rest for 5 minutes and then fold in the blueberries.
- Cook in your waffle iron according to your manufacturer directions.

Jessica Brooks

Toast With Refried Beans and Avocado

For the kitchen-phobic vegan!

Ingredients:

- 2 slices of your preferred bread
- 1 cup of vegan refried beans
- 1 thinly sliced avocado
- A few slivers of white onion
- Coarse sea salt

Instructions:

- Toast the bread until your desired level of doneness.
- Top with the refried beans and avocado.
- Add the slivered onions.
- Sprinkle with salt.

Banana Bread

Ingredients:

- 2 medium bananas
- 1/3 cup of brewed black coffee
- 3 tablespoons of chia seeds mixed with 6 tablespoons of water
- ½ cup of vegan butter
- ½ cup of maple syrup
- 1 cup of white flour
- 1 cup of wholemeal flour
- ½ teaspoon of salt
- 2 teaspoons of baking powder
- 1 teaspoon of cinnamon powder
- 1 teaspoon of ground allspice

Instructions:

- Preheat your over to 350F and life a loaf pan with baking parchment.
- Beat together the vegan butter and maple syrup until fluffy.
- Add the chia seeds.
- Stir in the mashed bananas and coffee well.
- Sift the flours, salt and raising agents and then gently fold into the wet mixture.
- Bake in the oven for 30-40 minutes, until brown on top and a skewer comes out clean.

Strawberry Shortcake Pancakes

Ingredients:

- 1 ¼ cup of whole wheat flour
- ½ cup of shredded, unsweetened coconut
- ¼ teaspoon of baking soda
- 1 teaspoon of baking powder
- ¼ teaspoon of ground allspice
- ¼ teaspoon of ground nutmeg
- ¼ teaspoon of ground cinnamon
- Pinch of kosher salt
- 1 cup of coconut milk
- ½ teaspoon of pure vanilla extract
- 1 tablespoon of maple syrup
- ¾ cup of warm water
- Extra-virgin olive oil
- 3 strawberries
- 1 frozen banana

Instructions:

- Preheat the oven to 250F.
- In a medium sized bowl, whisk the flour, coconut, baking soda, baking powder, allspice, nutmeg, cinnamon and salt.
- In a small bowl whisk together the coconut milk, warm water, maple syrup and vanilla.
- Add the second mixture to the first and whisk well until no lumps remain.
- Preheat a skillet over a medium temperature and add some extra virgin olive oil.
- Pour ¼ cup of the batter per pancake onto the skillet and shape them into circles with the back of a spoon.

- Cook until small bubbles appear and the bottoms of the pancakes are golden.
- Transfer the pancakes to a baking sheet and place in the oven.
- In the meantime, process the strawberries and frozen banana in a blender to make the cream sauce.
- Drizzle the sauce over the pancakes as well as maple syrup and serve immediately.

Egyptian Ful Madames

Ingredients:

- 1 pound of dried, dark brown marrowfat peas
- 4 cloves of garlic, finely minced
- 1 teaspoon of cumin
- 1 teaspoon of kosher salt
- A generous helping of extra-virgin olive oil
- 2 lemons
- A sprig of fresh oregano
- Pinch of ground black pepper

Instructions:

- Rinse and pick through the beans for any extraneous material, then place them in a bowl and soak overnight in water.
- Drain and add fresh water to cover the beans by about an inch.
- Bring to boil at a low temperature and cook until tender. It may be necessary to add more water.
- Drain the beans, but be sure to keep the cooking fluid as this will become your broth for your ful.
- Toss the marrowfat peas with the cumin, garlic, kosher salt and 2 tablespoons of extra-virgin olive oil.
- Place the beans into serving bowls and ladle the hot broth over the top.
- Drizzle more extra-virgin olive oil over the top.
- Garnish with a squeeze of lemon juice, the oregano and a pinch of black pepper.

Green Detox Smoothie

Ingredients:

- 1 cup of frozen strawberries
- ½ a cucumber
- 1 large banana
- 1 ½ cups of vanilla almond milk
- 1 cup of kale
- ½ cup of spinach

Instructions:

- Place all the ingredients into a blender and blend until smooth.
- Serve immediately.

Samoan Coconut Tapioca Porridge

Ingredients:

- 1 can of coconut milk
- ¼ cup of small-pearl tapioca
- 1/3 cup of sugar
- 1 ½ teaspoons of fresh lemon juice
- ½ cup of toasted unsweetened coconut flakes

Instructions:

- In a medium sized saucepan, place the tapioca and 2 cups of water.
- Let it soak for 30 minutes.
- Add the coconut milk and sugar, then bring the saucepan to a boil over medium heat, stirring constantly.
- Reduce to a simmer and cook for 15 minutes.
- Stir frequently to prevent scorching.
- Stir in the lemon juice and garnish with coconut flakes.

Chocolate Banana Nut Oatmeal

Ingredients:

- 2 cups of almond milk
- 2 large bananas, 1 ½ diced and the other ½ thinly sliced
- ¼ teaspoon of almond extract
- ¼ teaspoon of vanilla extract
- Pinch of kosher salt
- 2 cups of old fashioned rolled oats
- 2 tablespoons of unsweetened cocoa powder
- 2 tablespoons of agave nectar
- 1/3 cup of toasted and chopped walnuts
- Pinch of ground cinnamon
- 2 tablespoons of chocolate chips

Instructions:

- In a large saucepan over high heat, bring the almond milk, 2 cups of water, the diced bananas, almond and vanilla extracts and a pinch of salt to a boil.
- Stir in the oats, cocoa powder and 1 tablespoons of agave nectar and then reduce the heat to medium.
- Stir frequently for 7 minutes.
- Transfer to your serving bowls and top with sliced bananas, walnuts, agave nectar, cinnamon and chocolate chips.

Vegan Carrot Cakes

Ingredients:

- 2 cups of spelt flour
- ½ cup of sugar
- ½ extra-virgin olive oil
- ¼ cup of applesauce
- ½ cup of almond milk
- 1 pound of chopped carrots
- 2 teaspoons of baking powder
- 1 teaspoon of baking soda
- 2 teaspoons of ground cinnamon

For the frosting

- 4 ounces of Tofutti cream cheese
- 4 tablespoons of vegan butter
- 3 cups of powdered sugar
- 1 ½ cups of almond milk
- 1 teaspoon of vanilla extract

Instructions:

- Preheat your over to 350F
- In a food processor combine the sugar, oil and applesauce and pulse for 15 seconds.
- Using the shredder disc, shred the carrots into the mixture.
- Transfer the mixture into a mixing bowl.
- Add the dry ingredients and thoroughly mix.
- Fill cake jars, ½ way full or use a baking tray if you don't have access to jars.

- Place the jars in a shallow baking dish with ½ inch of water at the bottom.
- Bake for 25 minutes.
- Cool, and spoon a dab of frosting on top.

Country Style Fried Potatoes

Ingredients:

- 6 large potatoes, peeled and cubed
- 1/3 cup of shortening
- 1 teaspoon of salt
- ½ teaspoon of ground black pepper
- ½ teaspoon of garlic powder
- ½ teaspoon of ground paprika

Instructions:

- Heat a large cast iron skillet over a medium-high temperature.
- Add the potatoes and cook, stirring occasionally until the potatoes are a nice golden brown.
- Sean with salt, pepper, paprika and garlic powder.

Kale and Banana Smoothie

Ingredients:

- 1 banana
- 2 cups of chopped kale
- ½ cup of unsweetened almond milk
- 1 tablespoon of flax seeds
- 1 teaspoon of maple syrup

Instructions:

- Place all of the ingredients into a blender and blend until smooth.
- Serve immediately.

Berry Good Smoothie

Ingredients:

- 1 nectarine, pitted
- 1 cup of strawberries
- 1 cup of blueberries
- 1 cup of crushed ice
- ½ cup of almond milk

Instructions:

- Place all of the ingredients into a blender and blend until smooth.
- Serve immediately.

Flax Seed Smoothie

Ingredients:

- 1 frozen banana, peeled and cut into small chunks
- 1 cup of strawberries
- 2 tablespoons of flax seed
- 1 cup of low fat vanilla soy milk

Instructions:

- Place all of the ingredients into a blender and blend until smooth.
- Serve immediately.

Invigorating Banana Drink

Ingredients:

- 2 bananas
- 1 cup of almond milk
- 1 dash of ground cinnamon
- 1 dash of vanilla extract
- Ice

Instructions:

- Place all of the ingredients in a blender and blend until smooth.
- Serve immediately.

Black Melon Smoothie

Ingredients:

- 1 banana
- ½ a honeydew melon, cubed
- ½ cup of frozen blackberries
- 3 tablespoons of wheat germ
- 1 cup of almond milk
- Ice cubes

Instructions:

- Place all of the ingredients excluding the ice into a blender and blend until smooth.
- Divide the ice into glasses and pour the smoothie over the ice.
- Serve immediately.

Vegan Pina Colada Smoothie

Ingredients:

- 1 banana
- 1 cup of freshly chopped pineapple chunks
- ½ cup of coconut milk
- ½ cup of soy milk
- 1 tablespoon of agave nectar
- 1 tablespoon of ground flax seed
- 1 teaspoon of pure vanilla extract
- Ice

Instructions:

- Place all of the ingredients in a blender and blend until smooth.
- Serve immediately.

Avocado Banana Nut Smoothie

Ingredients:

- 1 cup of almond milk
- 1 avocado, peeled and pitted
- 1 large banana
- 3 tablespoons of creamy peanut butter
- 1 teaspoon of vanilla extract
- Ice

Instructions:

- Place all of the ingredients into a blender and blend until smooth.
- Serve immediately.

Jessica Brooks

Vegetable Muffins

Ingredients:

- 2 ½ cups of whole wheat flour
- 1 cup of cornmeal
- 2 tablespoons of baking soda
- 4 teaspoons of baking powder
- 2 teaspoons of chili powder
- 2 teaspoons of dried oregano
- 2 teaspoons of salt
- 1 ½ cups of grated carrots
- 1 ½ cups of chopped tomatoes
- ½ cup of finely chopped celery
- 1 clove of garlic, pressed
- 1 can of tomato soup
- ¼ cup of extra-virgin olive oil
- Freshly ground black pepper to taste

Instructions:

- Preheat your over to 375F.
- Grease 12 muffin cups.
- In a large bowl, whisk the flour, cornmeal, baking soda, baking powder, chili powder, oregano and salt together.
- Stir the carrots, tomatoes, celery and garlic into the mixture.
- In a separate bowl, whisk the tomato soup and extra-virgin olive oil together.
- Then, stir into the flour mixture until well combined.

- Spoon the batter into the pre-prepared muffin cups and sprinkle each muffin with black pepper.
- Bake in the over for around 15 minutes, or until lightly browned.

Groovy Green Smoothie

Ingredients:

- 1 frozen banana
- 1 cup of green grapes
- 1 cup of vanilla almond milk
- ½ a green apple, cored and chopped
- A generous handful of spinach leaves

Instructions:

- Place all of the ingredients into a blender and blend until smooth.
- Serve immediately.

Super Sweet All-Fruit Smoothie

Ingredients:

- 1 cup of blueberries, washed
- 1 sweet green apple, cored and chopped
- 1 small red apple, cored and chopped
- 1 cup of raspberries
- ¾ cup of white grapes
- 3 tablespoons of caster sugar
- Ice

Instructions:

- Place all of the ingredients into a blender and blend until smooth.
- Serve immediately.

Kinaja

Ingredients:

- 1 cup of freshly squeezed orange juice
- 2 kiwi fruits, peeled and sliced
- 3 ripe bananas
- 3 rings of pineapple
- Half a cup of fresh pineapple juice
- Ice

Instructions:

- Place all of the ingredients into a blender and blend until smooth.
- Serve immediately.

Save it for a Gloomy Day Smoothie

Ingredients:

- 1 mango, peeled and cut into chunks
- 1 banana, peeled and chopped
- 1 cup of freshly squeezed orange juice
- 1 cup of vanilla almond milk

Instructions:

- Place all of the ingredients into a blender and blend until smooth.
- Serve immediately.

Jessica Brooks

Golden Healthy Smoothie

Ingredients:

- 1 chopped carrot
- 1 banana
- 1 kiwi fruit, skinned
- 1 green apple, cored and sliced
- 1 cup of chopped pineapple
- Ice

Instructions:

- Place all of the ingredients into a blender and blend until smooth.
- Serve immediately.

Fruity Milkshake

Ingredients:

- 1 cup of pineapple chunks
- 1 banana
- ½ cup of frozen strawberries
- ½ cup of frozen raspberries
- ½ cup of frozen blueberries
- 1 cup of vanilla almond milk
- Ice

Instructions:

- Place all of the ingredients into a blender and blend until smooth
- Serve immediately.

Chery Tomato Pasta Salad

Ingredients:

- 300g pasta shells
- 3 cloves of garlic
- 6 tablespoons of extra-virgin olive oil
- 4 tablespoons of white wine vinegar
- 2 tablespoons of freshly chopped basil
- 2 tablespoons of freshly chopped chives
- 2 cups of cherry tomatoes, halved
- 1 cup of black olives, pitted and halved.
- Salt to taste
- Freshly ground black pepper to taste

Instructions:

- In a medium saucepan, cook the pasta with the garlic until al dente.
- Drain the pasta and set aside, reserve the garlic.
- Mash the garlic and mix well with the olive oil, vinegar, basil, chives, salt and pepper.
- Combine the pasta with the tomatoes and the olives.
- Pour the dressing over the top and toss well.
- Leave to stand for at least an hour.

Blood Orange Kale Salad with Almonds

Ingredients:

- 1 small bunch of curly kale, washed, dried and chopped
- 4 blood oranges
- 1 cup of chopped red bell pepper
- 1 cup of sliced almonds
- 4 tablespoons of extra-virgin olive oil
- 2 teaspoons of lemon juice
- 2 teaspoons of maple syrup
- Pinch of sea salt to taste
- Pinch of freshly ground black pepper to taste

Instructions:

- Remove the skins and as much of the pith from the oranges as you can.
- Cut three of the oranges into segments and leave the fourth aside for dressing.
- Combine the non-segmented orange, the extra-virgin olive oil, the lemon juice, the maple syrup and the salt and pepper in a blender and blend till fully mixed.
- Set the dressing aside
- Place the kale in a large mixing bowl.
- Massage the vinaigrette into the kale with your hands.
- Add the sectioned oranges, almonds and pepper to the salad.
- Re-mix and serve

Sweet Strawberry Salad

Ingredients:

- 1 ½ pounds of fresh strawberries
- 1 ½ tablespoons of dark brown soft sugar
- 1 tablespoon of balsamic vinegar
- ¼ teaspoons of freshly ground black pepper

Instructions:

- In a large bowl, toss the berries with the sugar and let it stand at room temperature for 10 minutes.
- In another bowl, combine the vinegar with the pepper.
- Pour this over the berries and toss to coat.
- Serve.

Chapter Five: 10 Lunch Recipes

Below you will find ten recipes that you can use for your lunches. Make sure you try different whole food items and spices to find a flavor that best suits your taste!

Avocado Salsa Salad

Ingredients:

- one cup of diced strawberries
- one cup of diced red onions
- ½ cup of cilantro
- one cup of diced tomatoes
- two cups of diced avocado
- greens

Instructions:

- Add one cup of diced strawberries
- Mix one cup of diced red onions
- Add ½ cup of cilantro
- Add one cup of diced tomatoes
- Add two cups of diced avocado

Mix together and sprinkle with pepper over your favorite bed of greens!

Chickpea avocado salad

Ingredients:

- 4 cups of cooked chickpeas
- one small red onion diced
- two minced garlic cloves
- juice of four limes
- one minced jalapeno pepper
- 1/2 cup of chopped cilantro
- 1 avocado
- Salt

Instructions:

- Combine 4 cups of cooked chickpeas with one small red onion diced, two minced garlic cloves, the juice of four limes, and one minced jalapeno pepper with the seeds removed, 1/2 cup of chopped cilantro, and salt. Mix these ingredients in a bowl and add one coarsely chopped avocado on top right before serving.

Tortilla soup

Ingredients:

- six corn tortillas
- seven large tomatoes
- two red bell peppers
- 2 cups of roughly chopped mushrooms
- one half yellow onion roughly chopped
- three cloves of chopped garlic
- 2 tablespoons of ground cumin
- two dried chipotle chilies
- five sprigs of fresh cilantro.
- 2 teaspoons of smoked paprika
- 1/2 teaspoon of chili powder
- salt to taste
- 2 cups of water
- 2 cups of fresh corn
- 2 cups of fresh green peas
- green onions
- cilantro
- avocado
- lemon juice
- corn tortilla chips

Instructions:

- Preheat your oven to 400°. Line a baking sheet with baking paper.
- Cut six corn tortillas into one order inch strips and spread them on your baking sheet. Cook them until they are crispy. This should take about 20 minutes. Then set them aside.
- Meanwhile place six large tomatoes cut in half with two red bell peppers cut in half, 2 cups of roughly chopped mushrooms, one half yellow onion roughly chopped, three cloves of chopped garlic, with 2 tablespoons of

ground cumin, two dried chipotle chilies, and five sprigs of fresh cilantro. Add 1 cup of water in a large soup pot and bring all of the ingredients to boil. Once boiling, reduce the heat to simmer and cover the pot for 20 minutes.

- When this is done remove the chilies and the cilantro sprigs. Transfer your soup to a blender and blend it until it is smooth, then pour it back into your pan. Add 2 teaspoons of smoked paprika and 1/2 teaspoon of chili powder to the mixture. Add salt to taste and 2 cups of water. Bring it again to a boil and then reduce the heat to medium for 10 minutes. Allow the soup to thicken.
- Add 2 cups of fresh corn and 2 cups of fresh green peas and cook until they are tender.
- To serve, garnish each bowl with green onions, cilantro, avocado, and tomatoes on top. Squeeze lemon juice lightly over the bowl and serve with your corn tortilla chips.

Vegetable Soup

Ingredients:

- vegetable broth
- ½ cup onions
- ½ cup peppers
- ½ cup carrots
- Parsley
- salt and pepper

Instructions:

- Bring vegetable broth to a medium heat on the stove
- Dice vegetables such as onions and peppers and carrots
- Add salt and pepper
- Let cook until the vegetables are tender

Let it cool appropriately and sprinkle with some parsley. Feel free to play around with the soup, add your favorite vegetables, it is bound to taste delicious!

Stuffed Portobello Mushrooms

Ingredients:

- Large Portobello mushrooms
- two cups of tomatoes
- fresh bay leaves
- coconut oil
- ½ cup onions
- ½ cup diced peppers

Instructions:

- Turn your mushrooms upside down
- Dice two cups of tomatoes
- Dice fresh bay leaves
- Sautee the tomatoes with coconut oil and onions and diced peppers
- Mix with the bay leaves
- Stuff into the mushrooms
- Place in the oven for ten minutes on 350 degrees

Let them cool and enjoy!

Tasty Bean Burgers

Ingredients:

- 1 large minced onion
- 1 minced garlic
- 1 tablespoon of paprika
- 1 teaspoon of cayenne pepper
- ¼ teaspoon of sea salt
- ¼ cup of almond meal
- 2 eggs substitutes
- ¼ teaspoon of pepper
- 1 pound of black beans

Instructions:

- Preheat your oven to 300 degrees
- Cook 1 large minced onion and 1 minced garlic in a pan on medium heat until they are soft
- Mix the onion and garlic in a bowl with:
    - 1 tablespoon of paprika
    - 1 teaspoon of cayenne pepper
    - ¼ teaspoon of sea salt
    - ¼ cup of almond meal
    - 2 egg substitutes
    - ¼ teaspoon of pepper
- Form inch thick patties with 1 pound of prepared black beans mashed into patty form
- Cook in a pan until brown on both sides

Then cover in mixture and place in the oven for 25 minutes.

Jessica Brooks

Chapter Six: 60 Dinnertime Recipes

Below you will find sixty recipes that you can use for your evening meals. Make sure you try different whole food items and spices to find a flavor that best suits your taste!

Black bean taquitos

Ingredients:

- one large yellow onion
- 1 tablespoon of water
- four cloves of minced garlic
- 2 teaspoons of ground cumin seeds
- two Chili's or 2 teaspoons of chili powder
- 2 to 3 cups of prepared black bean
- 18 corn tortillas

Instructions:

- Sauté one large yellow onion in a sauce pan for 10 minutes. Continually add 1 tablespoon of water at a time to keep them from sticking to the pan. Then add four cloves of minced garlic and cook for one minute. Add 2 teaspoons of ground cumin seeds and two Chili's or 2 teaspoons of chili powder. Add 2 to 3 cups of prepared black beans.
- Season the mixture with salt and then purée it until it is smooth with a little bit of chunk.
- Place 18 corn tortillas in a nonstick skillet over medium heat and heat them until they are softened. Stack the warm tortillas and wrap them in foil. Spread 3 tablespoons of your black bean mixture over each and roll them. Once you have prepared all of your tortillas,

place them in a large nonstick skillet and keep them for three minutes over medium heat. Service with a delicious tomato salsa.

Italian white bean soup

Ingredients:

- 1 cup of cannellini beans
- 4 cups of water
- one cube of vegetable bouillon
- 1/4 cup of water
- Four minced garlic cloves
- one half diced red onion
- two stocks of diced celery
- three stocks of fresh fennel
- one diced zucchini
- one bunch of chopped spinach
- 1 teaspoon of diced oregano
- Four chopped sage leaves
- 1 teaspoon of chopped fresh parsley
- sea salt and pepper
- lemon juice

Instructions:

- Drain 1 cup of cannellini beans and put them in a pot with 4 cups of water. Bring this to a boil. Then reduce the heat to simmer for 30 minutes until the beans are tender.
- Dissolve one cube of vegetable bouillon in 1/4 cup of water. Add four minced garlic cloves and one half diced red onion. Cook this while stirring constantly until the liquid has been released. Add two stocks of diced celery and three stocks of fresh fennel. Allow these vegetables to heat until they are lightly softened. Cover with 4 cups of water and bring to a boil. Simmer for an additional 10 minutes.
- Add your cooked beans as well as one diced zucchini, one bunch of chopped spinach, 1 teaspoon of diced oregano, four chopped sage leaves, 1 teaspoon of

chopped fresh parsley, and sea salt and pepper to taste. Cook this for five minutes on simmer until everything is cooked thoroughly and add lemon juice to taste and serve it hot.

Corn and black bean cakes

Ingredients:

- 1 1/2 cup of whole wheat pastry flour
- 1/2 cup of cornmeal
- 1 tablespoon of baking powder
- One half teaspoon of sea salt.
- 1 1/2 cups of unsweetened plant milk
- 1/4 cup of apple sauce
- one medium red bell pepper
- 10 ounces of fresh corn
- one cup of cooked black beans
- six green onions sliced

Instructions:

- Preheat your oven to 200°F.
- In a large bowl whisk together 1 1/2 cup of whole wheat pastry flour, 1/2 cup of cornmeal, 1 tablespoon of baking powder, and one half teaspoon of sea salt. Create a well in the middle of this mixture and add 1 1/2 cups of unsweetened plant milk, 1/4 cup of applesauce, one medium red bell pepper finely diced, 10 ounces of fresh corn, one cup of cooked black beans, and six green onions sliced. Fold these ingredients together with the dry ingredients.
- Heat your large nonstick pan and add a few drops of water to create a sizzle.
- Spoon 1/2 cup of the batter for each cake onto your skillet but do not let them touch one another. Cook until the underside is crisp and you can easily slip the pancake without it falling apart. Use a spatula to turn them over and cook the other side. You should cook them for about four minutes per side. You can serve these with a salsa or freshly chopped cilantro.

Jessica Brooks

Special mashed potatoes and gravy

Ingredients:

- 2 cups of vegetable broth
- 2 tablespoons of soy sauce
- 2 tablespoons of tahini
- 1/4 cup of brown rice flour
- freshly ground pepper
- four large Yukon potatoes
- two garlic cloves
- white pepper
- dash of sea salt
- 1/4 cup of unflavored plant milk

Instructions:

- To make the gravy:
    - Place 2 cups of vegetable broth, 2 tablespoons of soy sauce, 2 tablespoons of tahini, 1/4 cup of brown rice flour, and freshly ground pepper in a small saucepan. Cook over medium heat until it is smooth and thick and serve at once.
    - You can make this ahead of time and leave it in the refrigerator. To reheat it when you are ready to serve, add a small amount of water to a sauce pan and heat the gravy slowly.
- To make the mashed potatoes:
    - Peel four large Yukon potatoes and chop them into chunks. Place them in a stainless pan with water and cover them.
    - Add two garlic cloves and bring the mixture to a boil. Then reduce the heat and cover for 15 minutes until your potatoes are tender. Drain the water.

o   Mash the potatoes with a hand masher, electric beater, or immersion blender, and add white pepper and a dash of sea salt with 1/4 cup of unflavored plant milk until you get the smooth consistency you want.

Spinach potato tacos

Ingredients:

- two large potatoes
- one ten ounce package of frozen spinach
- one large diced onion
- one medium pepper
- 1 to 2 tablespoons of water
- two cloves of minced garlic
- 2 teaspoons of ground cumin
- 1 cup of unflavored plant milk
- 3 tablespoons nutritional yeast
- corn tortillas
- cilantro

Instructions:

- Place two large potatoes cut into small cubes in a medium saucepan and add water until it is covered. Bring this to a boil and then reduce the heat to simmer and cover it until the potatoes are tender. Drain them and set them aside.
- Meanwhile place a clean kitchen towel on your counter and place 1 10-ounce package of frozen spinach on it. Roll the spinach up in a towel and hold it over the sink to drain out as much liquid as you can. The same process can be used for fresh spinach that has been recently washed.
- In a large skillet cook one large diced onion with one medium pepper that has been seeded and diced. Add 1 to 2 tablespoons of water at a time to keep it from sticking to the pan. Add two cloves of minced garlic and 2 teaspoons of ground cumin to the mixture. Cook for one minute. Add your spinach and potatoes with 1 cup of unflavored plant milk and 3 tablespoons nutritional yeast. Season this to taste and cook it for 2 to 3 minutes.

- Meanwhile heat a large skillet over medium heat and add corn tortillas in a single layer. Heat them until the tortillas are warmed thoroughly. To serve, place your tortillas on a large platter and divide mixture in between. Sprinkle with cilantro and serve.

Vegetable stew

Ingredients:

- one large chopped onion
- two large chopped carrots
- two large chopped celery stalks
- 1 to 2 tablespoons of water
- three minced garlic cloves
- 1 tablespoon grated ginger
- 1 1/2 tablespoons of sweet paprika
- 2 tablespoons ground cumin
- 1 tablespoon of ground coriander
- 1 inch pieces of cinnamon stick
- 8 cups of vegetable stock or a low sodium vegetable broth
- one medium butternut squash
- one turnip
- one potato
- 18 ounces of crushed tomatoes
- 2 cups of cooked chickpeas.
- two large pinches of saffron
- 2 tablespoons of freshly chopped mint
- cilantro

Instructions:

- Place one large chopped onion, two large chopped carrots, and two large chopped celery stocks into a large pot and sauté them for 10 minutes. Add 1 to 2 tablespoons of water at a time to prevent them from sticking to your pan. Then add three minced garlic cloves; 1 tablespoon grated ginger, 1 1/2 tablespoons of sweet Paprika, 2 tablespoons ground cumin, 1 tablespoon of ground coriander. Then add two 1 inch pieces of cinnamon stick and cook for three minutes.
- Add 8 cups of vegetable stock or a low sodium vegetable broth, one medium butternut squash that

has been peeled and cut into small cubes, one turnip that is been cut into small cubes and one potato that has been cut into small cubes. Add 18 ounces of crushed tomatoes and 2 cups of cooked chickpeas. Bring this to a boil over high heat.

- Reduce the heat to simmer and cook for 25 minutes uncovered.
- Add two large pinches of saffron soaked in 1/4 cup of warm water for 15 minutes and 2 tablespoons of freshly chopped mint. Season your stew with salt and pepper and cook until your vegetables are tender.
- When you serve your stew top it with finely chopped cilantro.

Stuffed Avocados

Ingredients:

- 1 red onion
- 1 medium sized tomato
- 1 tablespoon of diced cilantro
- one avocado
- salt and pepper

Instructions:

- Dice 1 red onion
- Dice 1 medium sized tomato and remove the seeds
- Add 1 tablespoon of diced cilantro
- Slice an avocado in half and carefully remove the seed
- Add the mixture into the avocado

Sprinkle salt and pepper

Stuffed Peppers

Ingredients:

- one bell pepper
- black beans
- 1 small jalapeno
- one glove of garlic
- one tablespoon of cinnamon
- 1 tablespoon of cumin.
- one cup of wild rice or brown rice
- cilantro
- avocado strips

Instructions:

- Wash and cut bell peppers in half
- Remove any seeds and stems
- Meanwhile prepare black beans with 1 small jalapeno de-seeded and chopped finely, with one glove of garlic, one tablespoon of cinnamon, and 1 tablespoon of cumin.
- Prepare one cup of wild rice or brown rice and mix with cilantro when complete
- Add rice, beans, other vegetables such as onions to the bell peppers
- Top with avocado strips

Serve and enjoy!

Broccoli soup

Ingredients:

- 1 1/2 pounds of potatoes
- one medium yellow onion chopped
- 2 teaspoons of ground coriander
- 1 teaspoon of ground garlic
- 1 teaspoon of ground onion
- 1 teaspoon of poultry seasoning
- 6 cups of water. Bring this to a boil.
- 1 1/2 pounds of coarsely chopped broccoli
- three large Swiss chard leaves

Instructions:

- Combine 1 1/2 pounds of potatoes cut into chunks with one medium yellow onion chopped, 2 teaspoons of ground coriander, 1 teaspoon of ground garlic and 1 teaspoon of ground onion. Then add 1 teaspoon of poultry seasoning with 6 cups of water. Bring this to a boil.
- Reduce the heat to medium and add 1 1/2 pounds of coarsely chopped broccoli. Cook this for 10 minutes until you can feel the potatoes and broccoli are tender. Stir in three large Swiss chard leaves coarsely chopped and cook for an additional five minutes remove it from heat and let it stand.
- Blend the soup in the pot with an immersion blender until it is smooth with small chunks. If you do not have this type of blender you can ladle batches of your soup into a blender and process them gently. Then serve immediately.

Hummus filled potatoes

Ingredients:

- 15 ounces of prepared chickpeas
- two large garlic cloves
- 2 tablespoons of lemon juice
- black pepper and salt
- 1 tablespoon of cumin
- 2 teaspoons Dijon mustard
- zest of one lemon
- one half teaspoon of ground turmeric.
- 12 small red potatoes
- paprika
- small kale leaves
- green onions

Instructions:

- For the hummus, combine 15 ounces of prepared chickpeas with two large garlic cloves, 2 tablespoons of lemon juice, black pepper and salt to taste, and 1 tablespoon of cumin. Process this until it is smooth.
- In a small bowl Mix together 2 teaspoons Dijon mustard with the zest of one lemon, and one half teaspoon of ground turmeric.
- To make the potatoes steam 12 small red potatoes for 20 minutes and then plunge them into cold water. Slice each one in half using a small spoon or use a melon baller to scoop out a hole in the middle. Fill the hole with your hummus and mustard mixture and sprinkle paprika on top, garnish with small kale leaves or green onions.

Herb-Roasted Yukon Potatoes with Carrots

Ingredients:

- 2 tablespoons canola oil
- 1 tablespoon yellow mustard
- 1 teaspoon sea salt
- 1/4 teaspoon ground black pepper
- 1/4 teaspoon cayenne pepper
- 2 cloves garlic, minced
- 1 teaspoon dried basil
- 1 teaspoon dried rosemary, crumbled
- 1/4 cup dry white wine
- 1 ¼ pounds baby Yukon potatoes, thoroughly washed, scrubbed, and halved
- 1/2 pound baby carrots, halved
- 2-3 spring onions, sliced

Directions:

1. Preheat the oven to 400 degrees F. Prepare a suitable 8-inch baking dish.
2. In a bowl, combine oil, yellow mustard, salt, black pepper, cayenne, garlic, basil, rosemary, and dry white wine. Then, stir to combine and transfer to the baking dish.
3. Next, add the potatoes, carrots and onions to the baking dish.
4. Cover the dish with a foil and bake approximately 30 minutes.
5. Remove the foil and stir gently. Continue baking until the potatoes are fork-tender, or approximately 20 to 25 minutes. Serve immediately and enjoy!

Creamy Smashed Potatoes with Spinach

Ingredients:

- 1 pound frozen spinach
- 2 ½ pounds potatoes
- 3 tablespoons Dijon mustard
- 1/4 cup margarine
- 1/4 cup non-dairy sour cream
- 1 teaspoon garlic powder
- 1 teaspoon seasoned salt
- 1/4 teaspoon ground black pepper
- 1 teaspoon dried basil

Directions:

1. Cook the spinach according to the package instructions. Drain and reserve, keeping it warm.
2. Meanwhile, peel the potatoes. Next, cut the potatoes into bite-sized chunks. In a pot, boil potato chunks in a salted water until fork-tender. Drain the potato chunks and return to the pot.
3. Add the cooked spinach and remaining ingredients to the pot. Mash ingredients until the mixture is uniform and creamy, or until your desired consistency is reached. Serve immediately.

Quinoa Pilaf with Pistachios and Carrots

Ingredients

- 1 cup quinoa, rinsed and drained
- 2 tablespoons vegetable olive oil
- 2 tablespoons apple cider vinegar
- 1 teaspoon kosher salt, to taste
- 1/2 teaspoon ground black pepper
- 1 clove garlic, minced
- 3 tablespoon scallions, chopped
- 1 tablespoon fresh parsley, chopped
- 1 teaspoon ginger root, grated
- 1/2 teaspoon ground cumin
- 1/2 pistachios toasted
- 1 handful fresh cilantro, chopped
- 1 carrot, grated

Directions

1. Pour water into a deep saucepan and bring to a boil. Then, turn the heat to medium and cook the quinoa until it softens or for 10 minutes.
2. Next, drain cooked quinoa, fluffing with a fork and set aside.
3. In a large bowl, whisk the oil, vinegar, salt, pepper, garlic, scallions, parsley, grated ginger, and cumin. Mix well to combine.
4. Next, stir in reserved quinoa and pistachios. Scatter with the cilantro and grated carrot over the top and serve.

Grandma's Eggplant with Lentils

Ingredients

- 1 eggplant
- 1 tablespoon sesame oil
- 1 teaspoon sea salt
- 2 cloves garlic, minced
- 1 small yellow onion, finely chopped
- 1 teaspoon ground cumin
- 1/4 teaspoon red pepper, crushed
- 1/4 teaspoon ground black pepper
- 1 cup cooked lentils, rinsed
- 2 ½ cups water
- 1 tablespoon soy sauce
- 1 tablespoon vegan Worcestershire sauce
- 1 tablespoon fresh parsley, for garnish

Directions

1. Partially peel the eggplant and then cut it into thin pieces. In a large heavy skillet, heat the sesame oil over medium-high flame. Add prepared eggplant slices and season them with sea salt. Cook about 10 minutes, until the eggplant slices have browned.
2. Stir in the minced garlic and onions and cook 2 more minutes.
3. Then, add cumin, red pepper, black pepper and lentils. Cook for a minute longer.
4. Pour in the water and stir to combine ingredients. Add soy sauce, Worcestershire sauce and then bring it to a boil.
5. Cover, turn the heat to low, and simmer, until the lentil is tender and the water is absorbed, about 25 minutes. Stir occasionally.
6. Transfer your meal to a nice serving bowl, sprinkle with prepared parsley and serve with your favorite salad!

Sunday Spiced Rice and Beans

Ingredients

- 2 tablespoons canola oil
- 2 carrots, sliced
- 2 stalks celery, chopped
- 1/2 jalapeño pepper, minced
- 1 red bell pepper, seeded and diced
- 1 cup onions, chopped
- 1 teaspoon salt
- 1/2 teaspoon cayenne pepper
- 1/4 cup tamari sauce
- 2 ¾ cups vegetable broth
- 1 ½ cups long grain white rice
- 1 can (15-ounces) kidney beans

Directions

1. In a large-size pot, heat the canola oil over medium flame.
2. Add the carrots, celery, jalapeño pepper, red bell pepper, onions, salt and cayenne pepper. Then, cover the pot and cook for about 15 minutes, or until the onions are soft and the vegetables are slightly browned.
3. Next, add the tamari sauce and vegetable broth and deglaze your pot. Bring to a boil.
4. Add uncooked rice, bring to a boil again, and then reduce the heat to low.
5. Continue simmering for about 20 minutes. Drain the kidney beans, but do not rinse them. Then, add the beans to the pot and cook until the mixture is heated through. Serve!

Creamy Cheesy Pasta with Cashews

Ingredients

- 1 ½ cup eggless pasta of choice
- 2 cups non-dairy milk
- 1/2 cup non-dairy cream cheese
- 3 tablespoons cashews, chopped
- 3 tablespoons nutritional yeast
- 1 teaspoon sea salt
- 1/4 teaspoon cayenne pepper
- 1/4 teaspoon freshly ground black pepper
- 2 tablespoons extra-virgin olive oil
- 2 cloves garlic, minced
- 1/4 cup fresh parsley
- 1 tablespoon fresh cilantro
- Tomato ketchup for garnish (optional)

Directions

1. In a pot, cook the eggless pasta according to directions on a package. Drain the pasta, reserving 1/2 cup of the pasta cooking water.
2. Add the milk, cream cheese, cashews, nutritional yeast, salt, cayenne pepper and ground black pepper to a food processor or a blender. Process until the mixture is uniform and smooth.
3. In a cast-iron skillet, heat the oil over medium heat. Next, sauté the garlic, stirring constantly, about a minute. Add the cashew mixture and 1/2 cup of the reserved water. Bring it to a simmer and continue cooking until it becomes creamy and thick, approximately 8 minutes.
4. Remove the skillet from the heat and add the pasta. Stir in the parsley and cilantro and toss to combine.
5. Divide the pasta among four serving plates and serve with ketchup.

Nutty Rice with Beans

Ingredients

- 1 tablespoon olive oil
- 1 clove garlic, minced
- 1 ¼ cups brown rice
- 2 ½ cups water
- 1 bay leaf
- 1 teaspoon Himalayan salt
- 1/2 teaspoon black pepper
- 1/2 teaspoon red pepper flakes, crushed
- 1 tablespoon fresh parsley, chopped
- 1 tablespoon fresh cilantro, chopped
- 1 can (15-ounces) Great Northern beans
- 1/3 cup almond, roughly chopped
- 2 tablespoons margarine, softened
- 2 cups red onion, finely chopped
- 1 Roma tomato, diced
- 1 teaspoon lemon zest

Directions

1. In a wok or a large and wide saucepan, heat the oil over medium flame. Then, add garlic and rice, and stir-fry for 2 to 3 minutes.
2. Add the water, bay leaf and 1/2 teaspoon of the salt. Then, bring to a boil, cover with the lid, and simmer about 45 minutes, or until the rice becomes soft.
3. Reduce the heat to low. Add the black pepper, red pepper, parsley and cilantro. Drain and rinse the beans and add them to the pan along with chopped almonds. Stir to combine ingredients and reserve.
4. In a separate saucepan or a wok, melt the softened margarine. Sauté the onions until tender and

translucent or about 5 minutes. Add remaining 1/2 teaspoon of salt and stir to combine.

5. Add the tomato and lemon zest, and continue cooking for 2 to 3 more minutes. Pour this tomato mixture into rice mixture. Cook until heated through. Serve warm.

Creamy Country Noodles with Mushrooms

Ingredients

- 1 cup uncooked vegan noodles
- 1 tablespoon sesame oil
- 3-4 green onions, sliced
- 3 tablespoons all-purpose flour
- 2 cups vegetable broth
- 1 tablespoon tomato paste
- 1 ½ pounds button mushrooms, sliced
- 1/2 teaspoon seasoned salt
- 1/4 teaspoon ground black pepper
- 1/2 teaspoon garlic powder
- 1/2 teaspoon dried thyme
- 1 tablespoon fresh rosemary
- 1 teaspoon dried basil
- 1 tablespoon apple cider vinegar

Directions

1. Prepare the noodles according to the directions on the package until they are al dente. Set aside and cover, keeping the noodles warm.
2. In a wok or a large skillet, heat the oil over medium flame. Sauté the green onions until soft and translucent, or for 3 minutes. Add the flour and cook for 30 seconds, stirring often.
3. Gradually add the vegetable broth and tomato paste, stirring constantly. Continue to stir for about 1 minute until this mixture becomes bubbly.
4. Next, add the mushrooms, seasoned salt, black pepper, garlic powder, thyme, rosemary, and basil. Stir to combine ingredients.
5. Continue cooking for 5 minutes, until the mushrooms are tender and fragrant.

6. Add the apple cider vinegar. Turn the heat to low and cook for 4 more minutes. Finally add cooked noodles and gently stir to combine. Serve immediately.

Amazing Coconut Sugar Snap Peas

Ingredients

- 14 ounces water
- 1 can (14-ounce) coconut milk
- 2 cups uncooked wild rice
- 3 tablespoons fresh lemon juice
- 1/2 teaspoon sea salt
- 1/4 teaspoon ground black pepper
- 1 teaspoon dried basil
- 2 tablespoons sesame seeds, toasted
- 6 ounces raw sugar snap peas

Directions

1. In a large saucepan or a wok, combine the water, coconut milk and rice. Then bring to a boil.
2. Turn the heat to low. Continue simmering, covered, for about 20 minutes.
3. Remove the pan from the flame, remove the lid, and then add the lemon juice, salt, pepper and dried basil.
4. Fold in the sesame seeds and sugar snap peas. Stir to combine and enjoy warm or cold.

Easy and Healthy Mexican Quinoa

Ingredients

- 4 cups water
- 2 cups white quinoa
- 1 can (15-ounces) red kidney beans, drained and rinsed
- 2 cups corn kernels
- 1 cup chunky salsa
- 2 tablespoons extra-virgin olive oil
- 1 tablespoon lime zest
- 1 bay leaf
- Sea salt to taste
- 6-7 black peppercorns
- 1 teaspoon cayenne pepper
- 1 teaspoon dried basil
- 1 tablespoon fresh cilantro, chopped

Directions

1. In a large pot, bring the water to a boil. Add the quinoa, bring to a boil, then lower the heat, cover and continue cooking, for about 10 minutes, or until all of the liquid has been absorbed.
2. Remove the pot from the heat. Fluff cooked quinoa with a fork, and allow to rest for about 10 minutes in order to cool slightly.
3. Meanwhile, combine remaining ingredients in a large-size bowl.
4. Next, stir in the quinoa. Stir to combine ingredients. Serve with your favorite veggies such as tomato, bell pepper and onion. Serve hot or at room temperature, it's up to you.

Gnocchi with Herbed Tomato Sauce

Ingredients

For the gnocchi:

- 1 pound fingerling potatoes
- 2 tablespoons canola oil
- 1 cup all-purpose flour, plus more for dusting
- 1/2 teaspoon dried oregano
- 1/2 teaspoon dried basil
- 1 teaspoon garlic powder
- 1 teaspoon Kosher salt
- 1/4 teaspoon ground black pepper
- 1/4 teaspoon red pepper flakes

For the Sauce:

- 1 teaspoon extra-virgin olive oil
- 1 small onion, chopped
- 2 cloves garlic, minced
- 4 large tomatoes, diced
- 1/2 teaspoon salt
- 1/4 teaspoon black pepper
- 1/4 teaspoon cayenne pepper
- 1 teaspoon dried rosemary
- 1/2 teaspoon dried basil
- 1/2 teaspoon dried oregano

Directions

1. To make the gnocchi, preheat the oven 400 degrees F.
2. Prick a few holes in the potatoes with a fork. Place potatoes in a roasting pan and bake them for about 1 hour. Allow the potatoes to cool completely.
3. Discard the skins from the potatoes and add canola. Then mash the potatoes in a large bowl.
4. Add remaining ingredients for the gnocchi. Knead the batter until it is elastic and soft. Place the batter on a

well-floured surface. Divide the batter into 4 equal balls.

5. Next, roll each ball into a rope and cut each rope into 12 equal pieces.
6. Bring a pot of water to a boil and cook the gnocchi until they float to the top of the water.
7. To make the sauce, in a heavy skillet, heat the oil. Sauté the onions and garlic until they are tender and fragrant.
8. Then add remaining ingredients for the sauce and cook for about 15 minutes, stirring occasionally.
9. Divide the gnocchi among four serving plates, spoon the sauce onto the pasta and serve.

Saucy Spaghetti with Beans

Ingredients

- 1 tablespoon sesame oil
- 1/2 cup scallions
- 2 cloves garlic, minced
- 1 zucchini, grated
- 1/4 cup dried cranberries
- 2 teaspoons ground cumin
- 1 teaspoon cayenne pepper
- 1 teaspoon ground ginger
- 1 can (15-ounces) cannellini beans, drained and rinsed
- 1 can (15-ounce) tomato sauce
- 1/2 cup eggless spaghetti of choice
- 1 cup water
- 1/2 teaspoon kosher salt
- 2 tablespoon fresh parsley, chopped
- Kalamata olives for garnish

Directions

1. In a large-size saucepan, heat the sesame oil over medium-high flame. Then sauté the scallions, garlic, grated zucchini, and cranberries. Cook until the vegetables are tender, about 4 minutes.
2. Add the cumin, cayenne, ginger, and cook until fragrant, or for 1 minute.
3. Stir in the beans and tomato sauce, add the spaghetti and water. Add salt and stir well to combine.
4. Turn the heat to low and simmer for 15 minutes, stirring occasionally to prevent spaghetti from sticking to the bottom of the pot. Cook until the spaghetti are al dente.
5. Divide the spaghetti among four serving plates, sprinkle parsley on top and garnish with Kalamata olives. Enjoy!

Country Veggie Pie

Ingredients

For the crust:

- 1/4 cup hot water (100 degrees F)
- 1 teaspoons active dry yeast
- 1 tablespoon molasses
- 2 ½ cups whole-wheat flour, plus more for dusting
- 1 teaspoon kosher salt
- 1/2 cup salsa
- 1 ½ tablespoon olive oil

For the filling:

- 1 teaspoon olive oil
- 6 ounces soy chorizo
- 2 cloves garlic, grated
- 1/4 cup leeks, chopped
- 1 1/3 cup frozen green peas
- 1 cup salsa, store-bought or homemade

Directions

1. To make the crust, in a small bowl, combine the water, yeast and molasses. Stir to combine and let stand for about 10 minutes, until the yeast is completely dissolved.
2. In a large bowl, stir together the whole-wheat flour, kosher salt, salsa, and 1 tablespoon of the olive oil.
3. Add the dissolved yeast to the flour mixture and stir to combine. Transfer this mixture to a floured surface. Then, knead your dough 10 to 12 minutes, or until the dough is smooth and elastic.
4. Shape your dough into a large ball. Brush the ball of dough with the remaining ½ tablespoon of olive oil. Allow your dough to rise until it is double in size, or for about 90 minutes.

5. Meanwhile, make the filling. In a large heavy skillet, heat the olive oil. Then, crumble the soy chorizo into the skillet. Add the garlic and leeks. Cook over medium heat about 5 minutes.

6. Add the peas and salsa, lower the heat and simmer for 6 more minutes.

7. Preheat the oven to 375 degrees F. Coat a baking sheet with parchment paper or Silpat.

8. Punch airy, risen dough. Roll the dough out and shape it into an 8 × 10-inch rectangle on the coated baking sheet. Place the filling evenly on top and allow to rest for approximately 20 minutes.

9. Bake until the edges of the pie are golden brown, 20 to 25 minutes. Allow the pie to cool slightly before cutting and serving.

Amazing Italian Stuffed Peppers

Ingredients

- 4 medium red bell peppers
- 2 tablespoons canola oil
- 1 onion, chopped
- 2 clove garlic, minced
- 2 small zucchini, grated
- 1 ½ cups mushrooms, sliced
- 1 teaspoon cumin
- 1 tablespoon chili powder
- 1 teaspoon paprika
- 1 tablespoon fresh cilantro, roughly chopped
- 1 tablespoon fresh parsley, roughly chopped
- 2 cups whole-wheat breadcrumbs
- 1/2 cup vegan Parmesan cheese
- 1 teaspoon kosher salt
- 1/2 teaspoon ground black pepper

Directions

1. Core peppers, then discard seeds and all the white pith. Wash the peppers and then parboil them in boiling water for 3 minutes.
2. The peppers should stand upright in a baking dish, so, if necessary, cut a very small slice off the bottom of the pepper. Then rinse under the cold, running water, drain and set aside.
3. To make the filling: In a large heavy skillet, heat canola oil. Sauté the onion and garlic for about 2 minutes, stirring often. Add grated zucchini and cook another 3 minutes.
4. Next, add mushrooms and sauté another 1 to 2 minutes. Finally, add the rest of ingredients and cook for a few minutes longer, until the mixture is heated through.

161

5. Stuff prepared bell peppers with the filling. Arrange the stuffed peppers in the baking dish and bake at 350 degrees F for about 40 minutes. Enjoy immediately with your favorite vegan salad!

Quick Herbed Beans with Pasta

Ingredients

- 1 tablespoon olive oil
- 1 red onion, finely chopped
- 2 cloves garlic, minced
- 1/2 cup pecans, halved
- 1 (15-ounce) can kidney beans
- 1 bay leaf
- 1 teaspoon dried basil
- 1 tablespoon fresh sage
- 1 teaspoon dried thyme
- 1/4 teaspoon ground black pepper
- 1/4 teaspoon paprika
- 6 ounces cooked eggless pasta

Directions

1. In a wide saucepan, heat the oil and sauté the onion and garlic for a few minutes, until the onion is tender and fragrant. Add pecans and sauté for a few more minutes.
2. Drain the beans, reserving a small amount of the juice.
3. Add the beans to the saucepan, and cook, so the flavors can blend.
4. Next, add reserved juice, the spices and herbs and stir to combine. Cook until the beans are heated through.
5. Serve with your favorite eggless pasta, but any vegan salad might also work.

Mom's Chili Beans

Ingredients

- 1 tablespoon extra-virgin olive oil
- 2 tablespoons dry sherry
- 2 medium-size red onions, finely chopped
- 1 cup carrots, chopped
- 1 red bell pepper, thinly sliced
- 4 cups brown beans, cooked
- 1 cup water
- 1 cup vegetable broth
- 2 cloves fresh garlic, minced
- 1 large tomato
- 1 teaspoon celery seeds
- 1 teaspoon saffron
- 1 tablespoon chili powder
- 1/4 cup fresh cilantro, chopped
- 1 teaspoon agave nectar
- 1 teaspoon sea salt
- 4-5 black peppercorns
- Tortilla chips, crushed

Directions

1. In a large stockpot, heat the oil and dry sherry over medium flame.
2. Sauté the onions approximately 8 minutes. Stir in carrots and bell pepper and continue cooking another 5 minutes, stirring constantly. Add beans and stir to combine.
3. Next, add water, broth, garlic, tomato, celery seeds, saffron, chili powder, cilantro, agave nectar, sea salt, and peppercorns, and bring to a boil.
4. Cover with the lid, turn the heat to low and simmer for about 1 hour. Serve with crushed tortilla chips.

Creamy Mushroom Lasagna

Ingredients

- 2 tablespoons margarine or non-dairy butter
- 2 cloves garlic, minced
- 1 pound mushrooms, sliced
- 2 cups unsweetened soy milk
- 1/4 cup nutritional yeast
- 1 teaspoon dried oregano
- 1 tablespoon dried basil
- 1/2 teaspoon sea salt
- 1/4 teaspoon ground black pepper
- 1/2 cup all-purpose flour
- 12 lasagna noodles, prepared according to package directions
- 2 cups Tofu Ricotta

Directions

1. Preheat the oven to 350 degrees F. Have ready a suitable casserole dish.
2. In a medium-size skillet, melt the margarine or butter over medium-high heat. Then, add the minced garlic with mushrooms. Sauté until the mushrooms are tender and fragrant, for 5 minutes.
3. Add the soy milk, yeast, oregano, basil, salt, and pepper. Bring to a boil. Then lower the heat and simmer for 15 more minutes.
4. Combine the flour with 1/2 cup water to make a slurry. Slowly add the flour slurry and cook until it is thickened. Remove from the heat.
5. To make the lasagna: Place a thin layer of mushroom mixture in the bottom of the casserole dish. Then, lay 3 noodles, then place a thin layer of mushroom mixture, and finally place a layer of ricotta. Repeat until you run out of ingredients.

6. Cover and bake in preheated oven approximately 25 minutes. Uncover and bake for another 15 minutes.
7. Let the lasagna stand for at least 15 minutes before cutting and serving.

Eggplant Lasagna with Tofu Ricotta

Ingredients

- 2 eggplants, thinly sliced
- 2 ¼ cups marinara sauce
- 2 tablespoon fresh cilantro, chopped
- 2 tablespoon fresh parsley, chopped
- 1 tablespoon dried basil
- 1 teaspoon dried oregano
- 2 cups Tofu Ricotta
- 6 medium-size tomatoes, thinly sliced

Directions

1. Preheat the oven to 350 degrees F. Prepare a 9×13-inch baking dish.
2. In the bottom of the baking dish, place a thin layer of marinara sauce. Then, arrange the eggplant slices in a single layer. Again, place the marinara sauce over the eggplant. Sprinkle fresh cilantro over the eggplant slices.
3. Scatter Tofu ricotta in a thin layer. Sprinkle the parsley, basil and oregano over it. Add a single layer of tomato slices over the Tofu ricotta. Repeat this process with remaining ingredients. Finally, you will have 4 layers.
4. Cover with an aluminum foil and bake the lasagna for 30 minutes. Then, remove the foil and bake for 20 more minutes.
5. Allow to stand for about 15 minutes before cutting and serving.

Slow Cooker Vegetable Stew

Ingredients

- 1 tablespoon canola oil
- 3 garlic cloves, minced
- 1 onion, thinly sliced
- 2 medium potatoes, diced
- 1 tablespoon kosher salt
- 1 teaspoon celery seeds
- 1 tablespoon grated ginger
- 1/4 teaspoon paprika
- 1 cup vegetable stock
- 1 cup water
- 2 bay leaves
- 2 (15.5-ounce) cans chickpeas, drained and rinsed
- 1 red bell pepper, diced
- 1 medium head of broccoli, broken into florets
- 1 (28-ounce) can tomatoes with juice
- 1/4 teaspoon ground black pepper

Directions

1. In a saucepan, heat the canola oil over medium flame. Sauté the garlic and onion until translucent and fragrant, for 5 minutes. Add the potatoes and cook for a few more minutes.
2. Add the salt, celery seeds, grated ginger, paprika, and cook an additional 30 seconds to 1 minute. Pour in vegetable stock and stir well to combine. Transfer this mixture to a slow cooker.
3. Add the rest of ingredients, stir to combine ingredients. Then, cover and cook for 4 hours on high. Serve hot with your favorite ciabatta rolls, if desired.

Vegetable Coconut Sunday Chili

Ingredients

- 1/2 cup leeks, finely chopped
- 2 carrots, peeled and chopped
- 1/2 cup celery stalks, chopped
- 1 plum tomato, chopped
- 2 cups butternut squash, diced
- 3 large cloves garlic, minced
- 1 medium can of red beans, drained and rinsed
- 1 medium can of chickpeas, drained and rinsed
- 1 can non-dairy milk
- 2 teaspoons chili powder
- 1 teaspoon dried basil
- 1 tablespoon dried sage
- 2 cups vegetable broth
- 1/2 teaspoon kosher salt
- 1/2 teaspoon cayenne pepper
- 5-6 black peppercorns
- Chopped fresh chives, for garnish

Directions

1. Place all ingredients except the chives in a crock pot. Cook the chili on low heat for 8 hours.
2. In the last 1 hour of cooking, uncover the pot to allow the chili to thicken.
3. Divide among serving plates, scatter the chives over the top of chili and serve.

Winter Barley and Vegetable Chili

Ingredients

- 1 tablespoon olive oil
- 1 zucchini, finely diced
- 1 carrot, finely diced
- 2 cloves garlic, minced
- 1 large-size onions
- 1/2 teaspoon sea salt
- 2 tablespoons chili powder
- 1/2 teaspoon smoked paprika
- 1 teaspoon celery seeds
- 1 tablespoon dried basil
- 1 cup uncooked pearl barley, drained
- 3 cups vegetable broth
- 1 can (15-ounce) tomato sauce
- 1 can (15-ounces) pinto beans, cooked, drained and rinsed

Directions

1. In a deep and wide saucepan, heat the oil over medium-high heat. Stir in the zucchini, carrot, garlic, onion, and salt and reduce the heat to medium. Cook for 5 minutes.
2. Next, add the chili powder, paprika, celery seeds, and basil. Cook for 1 minute longer.
3. Add the barley, and cook an additional 2 minutes.
4. Add the broth and tomato sauce, and stir well to combine. Bring to a boil. Turn the heat to low, cover with the lid and simmer for 35 minutes, stirring occasionally.
5. Uncover the saucepan and stir in the beans. Continue cooking for 10 minutes over the low heat and serve warm.

Super Creamy Baked Macaroni

Ingredients

- Nonstick cooking spray
- 8 ounces whole-grain macaroni

For the topping:

- 1 cup bread crumbs
- 1/2 teaspoon kosher salt
- 1/2 teaspoon dried oregano
- 1 teaspoon dried basil
- 1 teaspoon dried rosemary
- 2 tablespoons extra-virgin olive oil

For the sauce:

- 1 cup nutritional yeast
- 2 tablespoons all-purpose flour
- 1 teaspoon onion powder
- 1 teaspoon garlic powder
- 1 teaspoon ground cumin
- 1 teaspoon kosher salt
- 2 cups unsweetened soy milk
- 1 tablespoon tahini
- 2 tablespoons margarine

Directions

1. Preheat the oven to 375 degrees F. Oil a baking dish with nonstick cooking spray.
2. Cook the macaroni following the package directions. Drain the macaroni, reserving 1/2 cup of the liquid.
3. To make the topping: In a bowl, combine all of the ingredients for the topping and stir well to combine. Set aside.
4. To make the sauce: In a saucepan, combine the nutritional yeast, flour, onion powder, garlic powder,

cumin, kosher salt, soy milk and tahini. Cook over medium-high heat, whisking frequently, until your sauce thickens.

5. Whisk in the margarine and stir to combine. Place the sauce, cooked macaroni and reserved liquid in the baking dish and stir to combine.

6. Spread the topping over the pasta and cover with an aluminum foil.

7. Bake in preheated oven for 20 minutes. Next, remove the aluminum foil and continue baking for 10 more minutes. Allow to stand for 10 minutes before cutting and serving.

Quick and Easy Seitan Crumbles

Ingredients

- 1/2 cup vital wheat gluten flour
- 2 tablespoons nutritional yeast
- 1 teaspoon agave nectar
- 2 tablespoons tamari sauce
- 1 teaspoon liquid smoke
- 1 tablespoon tomato paste
- 1 tablespoon margarine, melted
- 2 tablespoons water

Directions

1. In a bowl, combine the wheat gluten and nutritional yeast.
2. Stir in the agave nectar, tamari sauce, liquid smoke, tomato paste, margarine, and water. Crumble this mixture.
3. Cook in a saucepan over medium-high heat for 8 minutes.

Meat-Free BBQ Sandwiches

Ingredients

- 1 teaspoon extra-virgin olive oil
- 1 cup vital wheat gluten flour
- 1 tablespoon red pepper flakes
- 3 tablespoons nutritional yeast
- 1 teaspoon ground cumin
- 1 teaspoon garlic powder
- 1/4 cup natural peanut butter
- 1 cup water
- 1/2 cup barbecue sauce
- 6 vegan sandwich buns
- Lettuce leaves for garnish

Directions

1. Preheat the oven to 350 degrees F. Lightly grease a rimmed baking sheet with the olive oil.
2. In a large-size bowl, combine the wheat gluten flour, red pepper, nutritional yeast, cumin, and garlic powder. Then stir in the peanut butter and water. Stir until everything is well combined.
3. Divide this mixture into 6 portions. Shape them into 6 strips. Then, place the strips on the baking sheet.
4. Bake for 15 minutes, and then flip the strips and bake on the other side.
5. Drizzle the strips with barbecue sauce and bake for an additional 10 minutes.
6. Then assemble the sandwiches. Divide the strips among 6 sandwich buns, garnish with lettuce leaves and serve.

Vegetable Curry Delight

Ingredients

- 1 tablespoon sesame oil
- 1/4 cup scallions, chopped
- 2 cloves garlic, minced
- 1 tablespoon curry powder
- 1 teaspoon turmeric
- 2 teaspoons garam masala
- 1 tablespoon fresh parsley
- 1/2 teaspoon sea salt
- 1 ½ cups soy milk
- 1 tablespoon soy sauce
- 1 head cauliflower, broken into small florets
- 1 head broccoli, broken into small florets
- 15 ounces cooked green beans

Directions

1. In a large-size saucepan or a wok, heat the sesame oil over medium-high heat. Sauté the scallions and garlic until they are fragrant, for about 2 to 3 minutes.
2. Stir in the curry, turmeric, garam masala, parsley, and salt. Cook for 1 minute longer.
3. Pour in the milk and then add the soy sauce. Bring to a boil and add the cauliflower and broccoli. Lower the heat and then simmer for 15 minutes.
4. Add green beans and continue cooking for another 5 to 6 minutes.

Slow Cooker Sweet Potatoes

Ingredients

- 3 large-size sweet potatoes, diced
- 2 cups water
- 2 cups vegetable stock
- 3-4 spring onions, sliced
- 4 cloves garlic, minced
- 1/2 teaspoon Himalayan salt
- 1 tablespoon chili powder
- 1 tablespoon ground coriander
- 1 ½ cups red lentils
- 1 can non-dairy milk
- Chopped fresh cilantro for garnish

Directions

1. Put the sweet potatoes, water, stock, spring onions, garlic, salt, chili powder and coriander into your slow cooker. Then, cook on high for 3 hours, until the vegetables are just tender.
2. Add the lentils and milk to the slow cooker and stir to combine. Uncover the slow cooker and cook on high for an additional 1½ hours.
3. Sprinkle chopped cilantro on top and serve hot.

Smoked Lentil Sandwiches

Ingredients

- 28 ounces canned tomatoes
- 3/4 cup tomato paste
- 1/2 cup blackstrap molasses
- 2 tablespoon dry white wine
- 1 teaspoon lemon zest
- 1 yellow onion, sliced
- 2 tablespoon white vinegar
- 3 garlic cloves
- 1 tablespoon agave nectar
- 1 teaspoon dry mustard
- 1/2 teaspoon Himalayan salt
- 1/4 teaspoon black pepper
- 1/4 teaspoon smoked paprika
- 1/2 teaspoon dried tarragon
- 1/4 teaspoon liquid smoke
- 4 cups cooked lentils
- Vegan salad of choice

Directions

1. Put all of the ingredients, except the cooked lentils and salad, into a blender or a food processor. Process until the mixture is nice, uniform and smooth.
2. Transfer this mixture to a saucepan. Place the lid on the saucepan and bring to a boil over medium-high flame.
3. Next, turn the heat to low and simmer for 30 minutes longer.
4. Remove the saucepan from the heat and stir in lentils. Taste, adjust the seasonings and assemble the sandwiches, garnished with your favorite vegan salad.

Smoked Breaded Tofu Sticks

Ingredients

- 1 cup unsweetened soy milk
- 1 cup vegetable broth
- 2 cups smoked extra-firm tofu, pressed
- 3 tablespoons nutritional yeast
- 1 teaspoon salt
- 1/2 teaspoon ground black pepper
- 1 teaspoon dried rosemary
- 1/2 teaspoon paprika
- 1/2 cup all-purpose flour
- Vegetable oil for cooking
- Chopped fresh parsley for garnish

Directions

1. In a bowl, pour in soy milk and vegetable broth.
2. Cut smoked tofu into sticks. Place tofu in a bowl and set aside to soak.
3. To make the breading: In a separate small bowl, stir together yeast, salt, black pepper, rosemary, paprika and flour. Stir until everything is well combined.
4. In a large heavy skillet, warm the oil over medium-high flame.
5. Remove soaked tofu sticks from the bowl and squeeze them. Roll soaked tofu sticks in previously prepared breading.
6. Deep-fry tofu sticks in hot oil until they are crisp and lightly browned. Arrange fried tofu sticks on a serving platter, sprinkle with chopped fresh parsley and serve.

Mexican-Style Arepas Horneadas

Ingredients

- Nonstick cooking spray
- 1 cup tofu, drained
- 2 cups prepared polenta
- 2 tablespoons sesame oil
- 2 bananas, sliced
- 1 cup brown beans
- 1 large mango, seeded, and diced
- 1/4 cup scallions, diced
- 1 teaspoon sea salt
- 1/4 teaspoon black pepper
- 1/2 teaspoon paprika
- 1 chili pepper, minced
- 2 avocados, peeled, pitted, and sliced

Directions

1. Preheat the broiler. Grease a baking sheet with nonstick cooking spray.
2. Slice the tofu and polenta into slices similar to cutlets. Brush your slices with 1 tablespoon of sesame oil and place them on a baking sheet.
3. Bake the tofu and polenta cutlets under the preheated broiler 5 to 6 minutes.
4. Heat the remaining 1 tablespoon of sesame oil in a cast-iron skillet over medium-high heat. Fry the banana slices 5 to 6 minutes.
5. Put the beans into a blender and purée until a thick mixture forms. In a separate bowl, combine the mango, scallions, salt, ground black pepper, paprika, and chili pepper.
6. Place a slice of polenta on a serving plate. Next, place 1/4 of bean mixture on the slice of polenta. Lay a piece

of tofu, a few slices of avocado, a few slices of fried banana, and top with 1/4 of the mango salsa. Repeat with remaining ingredients. You will have four serving plates.

Meatless Sizzling Fajitas

Ingredients

- 1/4 cup canola oil
- 1/4 cup apple cider vinegar
- 1 teaspoon chili powder
- 1 teaspoon garlic powder
- 1 teaspoon dried basil
- 1 teaspoon dried oregano
- 1 teaspoon salt
- 1/4 teaspoon ground white pepper
- 1 small bunch fresh coriander
- 1 teaspoon molasses
- 3 zucchini, julienned
- 1 red bell pepper, sliced
- 1 red onion, chopped
- 2 tablespoons olive oil
- 1 (8.75-ounce) can corn kernels, drained
- 2 cups cooked chickpeas
- 1/2 lime
- 6 warm tortillas

Directions

1. To make the marinade. In a mixing bowl, combine canola oil, vinegar, chili powder, garlic powder, basil, oregano, salt, white pepper, coriander, and molasses.
2. Then, add the zucchini, red bell pepper, and onion. Place the bowl in the refrigerator and marinate veggies for at least 1 hour or overnight.
3. Heat olive oil in a large heavy skillet over medium-high heat. Sauté the marinated veggies until they are tender, approximately 10 minutes.
4. Turn the heat to high, stir in the corn kernels and chickpea, and cook until the vegetables are browned

and crisp-tender, for 5 minutes. Squeeze 1/2 of fresh lime and stir well to combine. Serve with warm tortillas and enjoy!

Potato Curry with Beans

Ingredients

- 2 potatoes, peeled and cubed
- 2 tablespoons extra-virgin olive oil
- 1/2 cup leeks, diced
- 2 cloves garlic, minced
- 1/2 teaspoon paprika
- 1 teaspoons ground cumin
- 2 teaspoons curry powder
- 1 rounded tablespoon garam masala
- 1 teaspoon sea salt
- 1 cup canned tomatoes
- 2 cups garbanzo beans, rinsed and drained
- 1 cup non-dairy milk

Directions

1. In a pot, place potatoes and cover with salted water. Bring to a boil over high heat. Then, turn the heat to medium-low, cover, and simmer about 15 minutes. Drain the potatoes and allow to steam dry for a few minutes.
2. Warm the olive oil in a skillet over medium heat. Sauté the leeks and garlic until the onion has turned translucent, for 5 minutes.
3. Season with spices and continue cooking for 2 minutes longer. Add the rest of ingredients and simmer on low heat approximately 10 minutes. Serve hot with your favorite salad on the side.

Chickpea Vegetable Stir-Fry

Ingredients

- 2 tablespoons peanut oil
- 1 teaspoon dried rosemary
- 1 teaspoon thyme
- 1 teaspoon dried basil
- 1 clove garlic, minced
- 1/2 teaspoon red pepper flakes
- 1/2 teaspoon ground black pepper
- 1 (15 ounce) can chickpeas, drained and rinsed
- 1 large zucchini, sliced
- 1 large carrots, thinly sliced
- 1/2 cup mushrooms, sliced
- 1 tomato, chopped
- 1 tablespoon fresh parsley, roughly chopped

Directions

1. In a wok or a wide saucepan, heat peanut oil over medium heat. Sprinkle with rosemary, thyme, and basil.
2. Add the garlic, red pepper, black pepper, chickpeas, zucchini and carrots, stirring well to combine ingredients. Cover and continue cooking for 8 to 10 minutes.
3. Stir in mushrooms and cook until mushrooms are fragrant and tender, stirring frequently. Lay the chopped tomato on top of the mushroom mixture.
4. Cover with the lid and allow the tomatoes to steam for a few minutes. Sprinkle with fresh parsley and serve immediately.

Perfect Shepherd's Pie

Ingredients

- 4 white potatoes, peeled and cubed
- 2 tablespoons margarine or nondairy butter
- 1/3 cup unsweetened dairy-free milk
- 1 teaspoon garlic salt, divided
- 1/4 teaspoon ground black pepper
- 1/4 teaspoon red pepper flakes
- 3/4 cup vegan kale pesto
- 2 heaping tablespoons chopped cashews
- 4 cups water
- 1 cup red lentils
- 1 tablespoon margarine or nondairy butter, softened
- 2-3 green onions, sliced
- 1 medium-size carrot, grated
- 1 medium-size zucchini, grated
- 2 plum tomatoes, diced
- 4 leaves fresh basil, minced
- 1 cup soybean cottage cheese
- Nonstick cooking spray

Directions

1. Place the potatoes in a pot, cover with water and bring to a boil. Next, cook approximately 20 minutes or until the potato cubes are fork-tender. Drain.
2. Add margarine or butter, dairy-free milk, 1/2 teaspoon of the garlic salt, black pepper, and red pepper flakes. Mash until the potatoes are smooth. Add the kale pesto and cashews. Stir to combine and set aside.
3. To a deep saucepan, add the water. Add the lentils and cook 15 to 20 minutes, until they are tender. Drain and reserve.
4. In a separate skillet, melt the margarine or butter over medium heat. Sauté the onions, carrot, zucchini,

185

tomato, and remaining 1/2 teaspoon of garlic salt. Cook until the vegetables turn light brown, about 5 to 6 minutes.

5. Stir in the basil, cooked lentils, and cottage cheese. Simmer additional 2 minutes.
6. Preheat the oven to 375 degrees F. Lightly grease a baking dish with nonstick spray.
7. Place the vegetable and lentil mixture in the bottom of the baking dish. Spread the mashed potato mixture over the top.
8. Cover with an aluminum foil and bake for 20 minutes. Then, remove the foil, and bake for 15 more minutes.
9. Allow the pie to stand for about 15 minutes before cutting and serving.

Flavor-Rich Crusty Tart

Ingredients

Nonstick cooking spray

For the crust:

- 1 ¼ cups all-purpose flour
- 1/4 teaspoon kosher salt
- 3 tablespoons tahini
- 1/4 cup plus 1 tablespoon water

For the filling:

- 4 cups water
- 1 cup brown lentils
- 1 tablespoon canola oil
- 1 small red onion, finely chopped
- 1 yellow or red bell pepper, thinly sliced
- 2 cloves garlic, minced
- 1 teaspoon kosher salt
- 1/2 teaspoon ground white pepper
- 1 teaspoon ground cumin
- 1/4 teaspoon paprika
- 1/2 teaspoon ground coriander
- 1/2 cup tomato sauce
- 1 tablespoon molasses

Directions

1. Preheat the oven to 375 degrees F. Lightly oil a pie plate with nonstick cooking spray.
2. To make the crust: Mix together the salt, flour and tahini in a food processor or with a mixer. Next, gradually add the water, 1 tablespoon at a time, and mix well to combine.
3. Shape the dough into a disk and roll out the crust. Replace the crust in the oiled pie plate. Gently prick the

crust, for instance with a fork, in order to prevent air bubbles.

4. To make the lentil filling: In a deep and wide saucepan, bring the water to a boil. Next, cook the lentils for about 25 minutes. Drain, and set aside.

5. In a separate saucepan, warm the canola oil over medium heat. Sauté the onion, yellow or red bell pepper and garlic for 4 minutes, or until the vegetables become tender.

6. Season with salt and white pepper. Then, sprinkle with cumin, paprika, and coriander, and continue cooking until fragrant or 1 more minute.

7. Stir in the tomato paste and molasses, and then add cooked lentils. Lower the heat, let simmer for 5 to 7 minutes.

8. Spread the lentil filling over the prepared crust and bake for 40 minutes, or until the filling is set. Allow the tart to rest for about 20 minutes before slicing and serving.

Nutty Mushroom Tofu Casserole

Ingredients

- 1 (15-ounces) can non-dairy milk
- 1 tablespoon curry powder
- 1 cup button mushrooms, chopped
- 1 ½ cup drained extra-firm tofu, pressed and crumbled
- 2 tablespoons cornstarch
- Nonstick cooking spray
- 2 cups soft wheat flour
- 1 tablespoon fresh parsley, chopped
- 1 tablespoon fresh basil leaves, chopped
- 1 teaspoon onion powder
- 1 teaspoon garlic powder
- 1/2 teaspoon sea salt
- 1/4 teaspoon black pepper
- 1/4 teaspoon cayenne pepper
- 1 tablespoon peanut oil
- 1 onion, chopped
- 1 can white beans, drained and rinsed
- 1/4 cup ground raw pecans
- 1/4 cup nutritional yeast

Directions

1. In a large heavy skillet, bring the milk with curry to a boil. Turn the flame to medium-low and then sauté the mushrooms. Add crumbled tofu and cook on low for 13 to 15 minutes. Then uncover and cook another 10 minutes.
2. Mix cornstarch with 2 tablespoon of cold water in order to make a slurry. Then, gradually add the cornstarch slurry. Mix until it is well combined.
3. Continue cooking until your tofu mixture is thickened or about 5 minutes. Allow this tofu mixture to cool slightly.

4. Preheat the oven to 350 degrees F. Prepare a casserole dish, by spraying lightly with nonstick cooking spray.
5. In a large-size mixing bowl, mix together the flour, parsley, basil, onion powder, garlic powder, sea salt, black pepper, and cayenne pepper.
6. Combine this flour mixture with tofu mixture. Knead the dough and set aside.
7. In a separate skillet, warm the peanut oil and then sauté the onion for a few minutes. Add the beans and cook for 5 to 7 minutes, or until the beans begin to brown.
8. Spread the dough in the bottom of the casserole dish evenly. Place the bean mixture on top of the dough. Scatter the pecans and the nutritional yeast all over the top.
9. Bake, covered with an aluminum foil, for 20 to 25 minutes. Then, remove the foil and bake for 10 more minutes. Allow to rest and cool slightly for about 10 minutes before slicing, and then serve.

Apple Gourmet Sausages

Ingredients

- 2 cups vital wheat gluten flour
- 1/4 cup nutritional yeast
- 1 teaspoon Himalayan salt
- 1 tablespoon dried basil
- 1 teaspoon onion powder
- 1 teaspoon ground cumin
- 1/2 teaspoon allspice
- 3 tablespoons peanut oil
- 1 ½ tablespoon pure maple syrup
- 1 cup apple juice
- 1 teaspoon lemon zest
- 1 cup unsweetened applesauce

Directions

1. Preheat the oven to 325 degrees F.
2. In a large-size mixing bowl, whisk together the flour, yeast, salt, basil, onion powder, cumin, and allspice.
3. In a separate medium-size bowl, whisk together the rest of ingredients.
4. Combine the dry flour mixture with the wet apple mixture. Stir to combine and then knead for a few minutes with clean hands. Let the dough rest for at least 5 minutes.
5. Roll the dough into 2 logs. Wrap in a foil and bake for 90 minutes. You need to flip the wrapped logs halfway through the cooking time.
6. Cut the sausages into halves and divide among four serving plates. Garnish with fresh sauerkraut and mustard and enjoy!

Amazing Sandwiches with Pumpkin Sausages

Ingredients

- 1 ½ cups vital wheat gluten flour
- 1/4 cup nutritional yeast
- 1 teaspoon cayenne pepper
- 1 teaspoon dried rosemary
- 1 teaspoon dried basil
- 1 teaspoon dried oregano
- 1/2 teaspoon ground black pepper
- 1/4 teaspoon ground cinnamon
- 1 teaspoon onion powder
- 1 teaspoon garlic powder
- 1 teaspoon agave nectar
- 3/4 cup vegetable stock
- 1/2 cup pumpkin purée
- 2 tablespoons peanut oil
- 2 sandwich buns

Directions

1. Preheat the oven to 325 degrees F. Prepare a baking tray.
2. In a large-size mixing bowl, whisk together the wheat gluten, yeast, cayenne pepper, rosemary, basil, oregano, black pepper, ground cinnamon, onion powder, garlic powder, and agave nectar.
3. In a separate mixing bowl, whisk together the vegetable stock, pumpkin purée, and peanut oil.
4. Pour the pumpkin mixture into the dry mixture, stir well to combine and then knead it for a couple of minutes. Allow to rest for 5 to 10 minutes.
5. Roll the dough into a log. Wrap in a foil and bake for 45 minutes. Then, flip the sausage and continue baking on the other side for another 40 to 45 minutes.
6. Make two sandwiches with vegan buns and enjoy!

Homemade Meatless Frankfurters

Ingredients

- 1/4 cup nutritional yeast
- 2 cups vital wheat gluten flour
- 1 teaspoon ground cumin
- 1 tablespoon garlic powder
- 1 teaspoon ground black pepper
- 1 tablespoon dried parsley
- 1 teaspoon tarragon
- 1 cup vegetable broth
- 1/2 cup sauerkraut
- 1/4 cup canola oil
- 6 boiled potatoes, for garnish

Directions

1. Preheat the oven to 350 degrees F.
2. In a mixing bowl, combine together the nutritional yeast, wheat gluten, ground cumin, garlic powder, black pepper, dried parsley, and tarragon.
3. In a separate mixing bowl, whisk together the vegetable broth, sauerkraut, and canola oil.
4. Next, combine the dry mixture with wet mixture and mix until everything is well combined.
5. Divide the batter into 12 equal pieces. Then, shape each piece into Vienna-style sausage. Wrap in an aluminum foil and bake for about 40 minutes.
6. Serve with boiled potatoes. You can serve as a hot dog.

Jessica Brooks

Savory Vegetable Muffins

Ingredients

- Nonstick cooking spray
- 2 teaspoons white vinegar
- 1 ½ cups unsweetened soy milk
- 3 tablespoons ground flax seed
- 1/4 cup water
- 1 cup cornmeal
- 2 cups all-purpose flour
- 1 teaspoon kosher salt
- 1 teaspoon baking soda
- 1/4 cup olive oil
- 1 teaspoon ground cumin
- 1 teaspoon onion powder
- 8 sun-dried tomatoes in oil, drained and chopped
- 1 yellow bell pepper, chopped
- 1 red bell pepper, chopped
- 4 small pickles, finely chopped

Directions

1. Preheat the oven to 350 degrees F. Lightly oil a 12-cup muffin pan with spray.
2. In a mixing bowl, mix together the white vinegar and soy milk.
3. In a separate small-size bowl, combine the flax seeds with water.
4. In a separate large-size bowl, whisk together the cornmeal, flour, salt, and baking soda.
5. Add the flaxseed mixture to the soymilk mixture, along with the olive oil, cumin, and onion powder. Fold this mixture into the flour mixture, and gently stir to combine. Next, fold in the tomatoes, bell peppers, and pickles.

6. Divide the batter equally among 12 muffin cups and bake until a toothpick inserted into the center of the muffin comes out clean, or for 18 to 20 minutes.

7. Transfer the muffins to a wire rack to cool before serving.

Creamy Bean and Tomato Soup

Ingredients

- 1 tablespoon canola oil
- 1 red onion, finely chopped
- 1 teaspoon garlic powder
- 1 teaspoon dried rosemary
- 2 carrots, chopped
- 1 stalk celery, chopped
- 2 tablespoons chili powder
- 1 tablespoon marjoram
- Sea salt to taste
- 1/2 teaspoon black pepper
- 4 cups vegetable broth
- 4 (15-ounce) cans black beans
- 1 (14.5-ounce) can crushed tomatoes

Directions

1. Heat canola oil in a large stockpot over medium-high flame. Add onion, garlic powder, rosemary, carrots and celery, and cook for 5 minutes. Season with chili powder, marjoram, salt and black pepper. Continue cooking for 1 minute longer.
2. Pour in vegetable broth, and then fold in 2 cans of beans. Bring to a boil.
3. In a food processor or blender, process remaining 2 cans of beans with crushed tomatoes until uniform and smooth.
4. Stir this mixture into boiling soup mixture, turn the heat to medium, and simmer for about 15 minutes. Serve hot with your favorite vegan croutons.

Saucy Tofu with Vegetables

Ingredients

- 1 tablespoon walnut oil
- 1/2 small head cauliflower, broken into small florets
- 1 small head broccoli, broken into small florets
- 1 green bell pepper, chopped
- 5 fresh mushrooms, sliced
- 1 pound firm tofu, cubed
- 1/2 cup nut butter
- 1/2 cup hot water
- 2 tablespoons tamari sauce
- 1 tablespoon pure maple syrup
- 1/2 teaspoon sea salt
- 1/2 teaspoon red pepper flakes
- 1/2 teaspoon paprika

Directions

1. In a wide heavy skillet, heat walnut oil over medium-high heat. Sauté cauliflower, broccoli, bell pepper, mushrooms and tofu for 5 to 7 minutes.
2. In a small mixing bowl, combine butter, hot water, tamari sauce, maple syrup, salt, red pepper and paprika.
3. Pour this mixture over vegetables and tofu in the skillet. Cook on low heat for 3 to 5 minutes, until the vegetables are tender and crisp.

Mushroom and Carrot Stuffed Zucchini

Ingredients

- Nonstick cooking spray
- 4 medium-size zucchini, unpeeled and halved
- 1 tablespoon walnut oil
- 4 green onions, chopped
- 2 cloves garlic, minced
- 2 large-size carrots, grated
- 1 cup mushrooms, sliced
- 1 teaspoon ground cumin
- 1 (15-ounce) can white beans, rinsed and drained
- 2 tablespoons apple cider vinegar
- 2 tablespoons chopped fresh parsley
- 1/4 teaspoon grated nutmeg
- 1 teaspoon sea salt
- 1/4 teaspoon ground black pepper
- 1/4 teaspoon cayenne pepper

Directions

1. Preheat the oven to 350 degrees F. Oil a shallow casserole or baking dish with nonstick cooking spray.
2. To prepare the zucchini "boats": Scoop out the flesh of the zucchini. Chop the zucchini flesh and set aside. Place the boats in the greased baking dish.
3. To make the filling. Heat walnut oil in a wide saucepan over medium heat. Sauté green onions for 5 minutes. Stir in minced garlic and sauté 2 minutes more, until it is lightly browned and fragrant.
4. Stir in the chopped flesh of the zucchini, carrots and mushrooms, and cook 5 minutes. Stir in remaining ingredients and cook a couple of minutes. Stuff the zucchini boats with prepared mushroom filling.
5. Bake until stuffed zucchini boats become soft, for about 40 minutes.

Mexican-Style Macaroni Skillet

Ingredients

- 1/2 pound eggless macaroni
- 2 tablespoons canola oil
- 3 spring onions, chopped
- 1 red or green bell pepper, chopped
- 1 (15.5-ounce) can chickpeas, drained
- 1 (14.5-ounce) can diced tomatoes
- 1 tablespoon fresh parsley, chopped
- 1 tablespoon white wine
- 1/2 cup corn kernels
- 1/4 cup olives, sliced
- 1/2 teaspoon kosher salt
- 1/4 teaspoon cayenne pepper
- 1/4 teaspoon ground black pepper
- 1/4 cup salsa

Directions

1. Bring a pot of salted water to a boil and cook the macaroni for about 10 minutes or until al dente.
2. Meanwhile, in a heavy skillet, warm canola oil over medium-high heat. Sauté spring onions and bell pepper until the vegetables are tender and lightly browned, for 10 minutes.
3. Stir in chickpeas, tomatoes, parsley, wine, corn kernels, olives, salt, cayenne pepper, black pepper and salsa. Cook until your sauce is thoroughly heated, or 5 to 7 minutes.
4. Toss the sauce with the macaroni and serve with some extra olives and your favorite salad.

Herbed and Stewed Summer Vegetables

Ingredients

- 1/2 cup extra-virgin olive oil
- 2 shallots, thinly sliced
- 2 cloves garlic, minced
- 2 zucchini, peeled and diced
- 1 stalk celery, chopped
- 1 large-size carrot, sliced
- 1 medium eggplant, cubed
- 1 yellow squash, cubed
- 2 red bell peppers, chopped
- 1 jalapeño pepper, minced
- 4 medium-size tomatoes, peeled and diced
- 1 tablespoon fresh parsley, roughly chopped
- 1 tablespoon fresh cilantro, roughly chopped
- 1 teaspoon sea salt
- 1/2 teaspoon black pepper
- 1/2 teaspoon paprika

Directions

1. In a large pot over medium-low heat, cook the shallots and garlic in 1 ½ tablespoon of hot olive oil. Cook until tender and translucent.
2. In a wok or a wide skillet, heat 1 ½ tablespoon of olive oil and sauté the zucchini until they are slightly browned. Add the zucchini to the pot with the shallots and garlic.
3. Add remaining olive oil and add celery, carrot, eggplant, squash, bell peppers, and jalapeño pepper. Cook over medium heat for 20 minutes longer. Replace to the pot.
4. Add the tomatoes to the pot, sprinkle with herbs and spices and cook another 12 to 15 minutes, stirring occasionally. Taste, adjust the seasonings and serve hot.

Tangy BBQ Sandwiches with Tempeh

Ingredients

- 1 cup vegan BBQ sauce
- 1 cup tempeh, crumbled
- 1 tablespoon extra-virgin olive oil
- 1 medium leek, finely chopped
- 1 large-size carrot, cut into strips
- 2 red or green bell peppers, thinly sliced
- 4 sandwich rolls, split
- 1 teaspoon mustard
- 8-10 iceberg lettuce leaves, drizzled with lemon juice

Directions

1. Into a medium-size bowl, pour the BBQ sauce of your choice. Place the tempeh in the bowl, and let it marinate about 10 to 15 minutes.
2. Heat olive oil in a cast-iron skillet over medium heat. Add the leek, carrot, and sliced bell peppers.
3. Cook, stirring often, until the vegetables are tender. Stir in the marinated tempeh together with sauce, and cook until it is heated through.
4. Spoon the tempeh with vegetables onto sandwich rolls, garnish with mustard and iceberg lettuce and serve.

Colorful Mushroom Vegetable Pilaf

Ingredients

- 1 tablespoon canola oil
- 4 spring onions, chopped
- 4 cloves garlic, minced
- 1 cup quinoa, rinsed
- 1 cup half cooked wild rice
- 1 cup canned lentils, rinsed
- 2 medium-size carrots
- 2 stalks celery, chopped
- 1 cup fresh mushrooms, chopped
- 1 quart vegetable broth
- 1 teaspoon dried basil
- 1 teaspoon dried rosemary
- 1 bunch kale, stems removed
- 1 teaspoon fine sea salt
- 1/4 teaspoon ground white pepper
- 1/4 teaspoon cayenne pepper
- 1 tablespoon fresh parsley, chopped

Directions

1. In a large-size pot, warm canola oil over medium heat. Stir in the spring onions and garlic, and sauté 5 minutes, until spring onions are translucent and tender.
2. Stir in quinoa, wild rice, lentils, carrots, celery, and mushrooms. Pour in the vegetable broth, cover with the lid and cook for about 10 minutes. Season with basil and rosemary and continue cooking another 10 minutes.
3. Turn off the stove and add remaining ingredients to the pot. Place the lid, and allow to stand for 8 to 10 minutes, until kale is wilted.

Mediterranean Veggie Couscous

Ingredients

- 1 cup water
- 1 cup sun-dried tomatoes, dehydrated
- 1/2 (10-ounce) package couscous
- 1 teaspoon sesame oil
- 3 cloves garlic, pressed
- 1 large red onion, finely chopped
- 1 carrot, shredded
- 1/3 cup fresh basil leaves
- Juice of 1/2 fresh lemon
- 1/2 teaspoon sea salt
- 1/4 teaspoon black pepper
- 1/4 teaspoon cayenne pepper
- 1/2 cup mushroom, sliced
- Sliced olives for garnish

Directions

1. Pour the water into a bowl. Then place the sun-dried tomatoes in a bowl and soak them for 30 minutes. Remove rehydrated tomatoes from the water, drain and chop them. Reserve the tomato water.
2. In a deep saucepan, combine the reserved tomato water with 1/2 cup of water. Bring to a boil and cook the couscous. Remove from the flame and allow to sit for 5 minutes, until liquid has been absorbed. Then fluff the couscous with a fork.
3. In a heavy skillet, heat the sesame oil over medium heat. Next, stir in the reserved and rehydrated sun-dried tomatoes, garlic, and red onion.
4. Cook about 5 minutes, stirring frequently, until the onions are translucent, fragrant and tender. Mix in the carrot, basil, and lemon juice. Season with sea salt, black pepper, and cayenne.

5. Stir in the mushrooms, and continue cooking for 5 minutes. Stir occasionally. Toss this mixture with the couscous, taste, adjust the seasonings and transfer to the serving platter. Garnish with olives and serve immediately.

Easy Portobello Mushroom Pasta

Ingredients

- 5 tablespoons canola oil
- 1 small bunch spring onions, chopped
- 4 cloves garlic, minced
- 4 Roma tomatoes, diced
- 1 large-size carrot, thinly sliced
- 1 cup Portobello mushrooms, sliced
- 1 teaspoon dried basil
- 1/2 teaspoon dried oregano
- 1 teaspoon dried rosemary
- 1 tablespoon cilantro
- 1 teaspoon sea salt
- 1/4 teaspoon black pepper
- 1/4 teaspoon paprika
- 1 pound eggless pasta of choice

Directions

1. In a medium-size heavy skillet, heat the oil over medium-high heat. Then sauté spring onions and garlic for 2 to 4 minutes, until they are just tender and fragrant.
2. Stir in tomatoes, carrot and mushrooms, and cook 5 minutes until the carrot becomes slightly soft. Next, sprinkle with basil, oregano, rosemary, cilantro, sea salt, black pepper, and paprika.
3. Next, reduce the heat to low and let simmer for 10 minutes longer.
4. Bring a pot of lightly salted water to a boil and cook your favorite pasta. Cook approximately 5 minutes, until al dente.
5. Toss drained pasta with sauce and divide among four serving plates. You can garnish with crumbled tofu, olives, ketchup, it's up to you.

Super Healthy Vegetable Rice Stew

Ingredients

- 1 eggplant, peeled and sliced
- 1 teaspoon sea salt
- 1/4 cup canola oil
- 1 cup leeks, chopped
- 4 cloves garlic, crushed
- 1/2 cup brown rice
- 1 green bell pepper, thinly sliced
- 1 red bell pepper, thinly sliced
- 3 fresh tomatoes, diced
- 1 ½ cups water
- 2 tablespoons sherry vinegar
- 1/2 teaspoon salt
- 1/4 teaspoon ground black pepper
- 1/4 teaspoon red pepper flakes
- 1/4 cup fresh basil leaves, chopped
- 1 sprig fresh rosemary, chopped
- 1 tablespoon fresh cilantro, chopped
- 1 tablespoon fresh parsley, chopped
- 1 bay leaf

Directions

1. Sprinkle the slices of eggplant with 1 teaspoon of salt. Place slices of eggplant in a colander and allow to stand for about 30 minutes. Rinse the slices of eggplant and pat dry.
2. Heat canola oil in a large pot over medium heat. Sauté eggplant until slightly browned. Then, add leeks and sauté until fragrant and tender, for 5 minutes. Add the garlic and sauté for 2 to 3 minutes longer.
3. Stir in brown rice, green bell pepper, red bell pepper, tomatoes, water, sherry vinegar, salt, black pepper, and red pepper flakes. Turn the heat to medium-high and cook for about 10 minutes. Turn the heat to medium-

low and simmer for 45 minutes, or until vegetables become soft.

4. Remove the pot from the heat and stir in basil, rosemary, cilantro, parsley, and bay leaf. Enjoy immediately!

Peppery Seitan Fajitas

Ingredients

- 2 tablespoons extra-virgin olive oil
- 1 small onion, finely chopped
- 2 red bell pepper, thinly sliced
- 1 green bell pepper, thinly sliced
- 1 jalapeño pepper, seeded and minced
- 1 pound seitan, cut into strips
- 2 tablespoons tamari sauce
- 3 cloves garlic, minced
- 1 teaspoon smoked paprika
- 1/4 teaspoon ground black pepper
- 1 teaspoon turmeric
- 1 teaspoon ground cumin
- 1/2 teaspoon kosher salt
- 10 whole grain vegan tortillas

Directions

1. To make the filling: Heat olive oil in a large heavy skillet over medium heat. Cook the onion, bell peppers, and jalapeño pepper, until they become tender, about 5 minutes.
2. Add seitan, tamari sauce, garlic, smoked paprika, black pepper, turmeric, and ground cumin. Turn the heat to low. Season with salt and continue cooking for 10 minutes longer.
3. Warm the tortillas. Spoon seitan filling onto each tortilla and fold the tortillas.

Chapter Seven: 10 Snack/Appetizer Recipes

Below you will find ten recipes that you can use for a snack. Make sure you try different whole food items and spices to find a flavor that best suits your taste!

Spinach and peach green smoothie

Ingredients:

- one frozen peach
- one cup of washed spinach
- one cup of almond milk
- one tray of ice

Instructions:

- Add one frozen peach
- Add one cup of washed spinach
- Add one cup of almond milk
- Add one tray of ice

Blend until creamy and enjoy!

Green smoothie with kiwi and kale

Ingredients:

- one cup of washed kale
- one kiwi with the skin peeled
- one cup of almond milk
- two tablespoons of agave nectar
- one tray of ice

Instructions:

- Add one cup of washed kale
- Add one kiwi with the skin peeled
- Add one cup of almond milk
- Add two tablespoons of agave nectar
- Add one tray of ice

Tropical De-Stress Smoothie

Ingredients:

- one cup of pineapple
- one cup of mangoes
- one frozen banana
- one cup of almond milk
- one tablespoon of lime juice
- one tray of ice

Instructions:

- Add one cup of pineapple
- Add one cup of mangoes
- Add one frozen banana
- Add one cup of almond milk
- Add one tablespoon of lime juice
- Add one tray of ice

Blend until creamy and enjoy

Strawberry and banana smoothie

Ingredients:

- one frozen banana
- one cup of strawberries (leave the stem for added benefits)
- one cup of almond milk
- two tablespoons of agave nectar
- one tray of ice

Instructions:

- Add one frozen banana
- Add one cup of strawberries
- Add one cup of almond milk
- Add two tablespoons of agave nectar
- Add one tray of ice

Blend until creamy and enjoy!

Detox Green Smoothie

Ingredients:

- two cups of spinach
- one cup of kale
- one diced banana
- one diced green apple
- one cup of fresh orange juice
- one tray of ice

Instructions:

- Add two cups of spinach
- Add one cup of kale
- Add one diced banana
- Add one diced green apple
- Add one cup of fresh orange juice
- Add one tray of ice

Blend until creamy and enjoy!

Jessica Brooks

Pink smoothie

Ingredients:

- one frozen banana
- one cup of strawberries (leave the stem for added benefits)
- one cup of almond milk
- two tablespoons of agave nectar
- one cup of peanuts
- one tray of ice

Instructions:

- Add one frozen banana
- Add one cup of strawberries
- Add one cup of almond milk
- Add two tablespoons of agave nectar
- Add one cup of peanuts
- Add one tray of ice

Blend until creamy and enjoy!

Peach Protein smoothie

Ingredients:

- one peach
- one frozen banana
- ¼ cup of coconut cream
- 1 cup of water
- 30 grams of vegan protein substitute powder
- 1 tray of ice

Instructions:

- Wash and quarter one peach; remove the seed
- Add one frozen banana
- Add ¼ cup of coconut cream
- Add 1 cup of water
- Add 30 grams of protein
- Add 1 tray of ice

Blend until smoothie and creamy!

Coleslaw

Ingredients:

- 1 tablespoon of olive oil
- 1 teaspoon of agave nectar
- 1/4 teaspoon of salt
- ¼ teaspoon of pepper
- ¼ teaspoon of ground mustard seed
- 1/8 teaspoon of cumin seed
- 2 tablespoons of apple cider vinegar
- 1 small red cabbage

Instructions:

- Mix in a large bowl:
    - 1 tablespoon of olive oil
    - 1 teaspoon of agave nectar
    - 1/4 teaspoon of salt
    - ¼ teaspoon of pepper
    - ¼ teaspoon of ground mustard seed
    - 1/8 teaspoon of cumin seed
    - 2 tablespoons of apple cider vinegar
- Shred 1 small red cabbage and place in a separate bowl
- Add dressing to the cabbage and mix

Serve immediately

Pear Appetizer

Ingredients

- Pears
- Pancetta slices
- Agave nectar

Instructions:

- Dice pears into small circular slices
- Add a circular piece of pancetta on each pear slice
- Sprinkle with raw agave nectar

Bring out at parties and enjoy!

Tomato salsa

Ingredients:
- 1 dried red chili
- 6 tomatoes
- 1 garlic clove
- 1 onion wedge
- 1 tablespoon fresh cilantro
- Sea salt
- Oil free tortilla chips

Instructions:
- Place one piece of dried red chili in a skillet and cook on high for one minute until it begins to puff. Do not burn the chili! Remove it from your pan and set it aside.
- Place six ripe and plum tomatoes whole in your skillet and roast them over medium heat. Turn them to prevent charring and roast them until the entire surface is lightly charred. This should take about 10 minutes. Remove them from the pan and set them aside to cool.
- Place two of your tomatoes in a blender with your roasted chili, one garlic clove, and onion wedges. Add salt to taste. Blend this into a smooth sauce and add the remaining tomatoes until it is a chunky purée. Stir in 1 tablespoon of finely chopped fresh cilantro. Adjust the seasoning to your liking.
- Transfer to a bowl and chill until you are ready to serve. Enjoy this also with oil free tortilla chips.

Chapter Ten: 10 Sauce, Dip and Condiments Recipes

Below you will find ten recipes that you can use to create vegan friendly sauces, dips and condiments. Make sure you try different whole food items and spices to find a flavor that best suits your taste!

Vegan Hummus

Ingredients:
- 2 cups of chickpeas
- Teaspoon of fresh lemon juice
- 3 tablespoon olive oil
- 3 tablespoons of water
- 1 garlic clove, minced
- 3 tablespoons of tahini
- ½ teaspoon of cumin
- Salt and pepper to taste

Instructions:

- Simply place all of the ingredients into a blender and blend until as smooth as possible. You may need to add additional water to achieve the right smoothness. Be sure to experiment with this recipe and try sprinkling in some paprika or olive oil before serving.

Broccoli Guacamole

Ingredients:
- 1 cup of broccoli, as finely chopped as possible
- 2 diced avocadoes
- 1 diced tomato
- ¼ cup of minced red onion
- 1 clove of garlic
- 1 tablespoon of lemon juice
- Cilantro
- Salt to taste

Instructions:
- Mix all of the ingredients together, except for the avocadoes.
- Gently fold the avocado chunks into the mixture
- Season with a tiny amount of salt, if needed.

Rocket and Cashew Spread

Ingredients:
- 1.5 cups raw cashew nuts
- 1 clove of garlic
- 2 cups of rocket
- ¼ cup of nutritional yeast
- 2 tablespoons of lemon juice
- ¼ cup of extra virgin olive oil
- Salt and pepper to taste

Instructions:
- Place the cashew nuts, nutritional yeast and a clove of garlic into a food processor and pulse it gently until the ingredients are all mixed but the cashews are still chunky. Place into a bowl and set aside.
- Blend the olive oil and lemon juice, followed by the rocket and then mix this mixture into the cashew mixture.
- Season with salt and pepper.
- Serve with crostini type crackers!

Vegan Pesto

Ingredients:
- ½ cup of lightly toasted pine nuts
- 2 cups of fresh basil
- ½ cup of extra virgin olive oil
- 1 clove of garlic, minced
- 2 teaspoons of lemon juice
- Salt and pepper to taste

Instructions:
- Blend all of the ingredients together in a food processor or immersion blender.
- Serve immediately.
- Can be frozen for up to 3 months

Cashew Mayonnaise

Ingredients:
- 2 tablespoons of flaxseed oil
- 2 tablespoons of extra virgin olive oil
- 1 cup of raw cashew nuts
- ¼ cup of water
- ¼ cup of fresh lemon juice
- 2 soft pitted medjool dates
- 1 teaspoon of salt
- 1 teaspoon of onion powder
- ½ teaspoon of garlic powder
- Pinch of ground black pepper

Instructions:
- Soak the cashew nuts for 2 hours and then drain.
- Combine the cashew nuts, water, salt and pepper, garlic and onion powder, dates and lemon juice in a blender and blend until smooth.
- Add the extra virgin olive oil and the flaxseed oil to the mixture and blend until emulsified.
- If you find the mixture becomes too thick, add a teaspoon of water at a time until it softens up.

Creamy Cauliflower Herb Salad Dressing

Ingredients:
- 1 cup of raw cauliflower florets
- 1 cup of water
- The juice of one whole lemon, 2 tablespoons worth
- 1 clove of garlic, peeled and minced
- 2 teaspoons of extra virgin olive oil
- 2 teaspoons of agave nectar
- 1 teaspoon of brown mustard
- 1 teaspoon of apple cider vinegar
- Salt and pepper to taste
- 2 tablespoons of fresh basil

Instructions:
- Roast the garlic with oil at a low temperature until the garlic is soft in a small frying pan.
- Put the cauliflower and water together in a pot and bring to boil. Cover and cook the cauliflower at a low temperature until it is tender. This should take roughly ten minutes.
- Chop up the basil.
- Add the contents of the pot into a blender and add the roasted garlic, lemon juice, mustard, apple cider vinegar, agave nectar. Add the salt and pepper to taste.
- Blend until creamy and smooth. Add a teaspoon or two of water if needed.
- Goes perfectly with a spinach salad.

Mango Chutney

Ingredients:
- ¼ teaspoon of curry powder
- 2 teaspoons of peanut oil
- 2 cloves of garlic, minced
- 2 tablespoons of red wine vinegar
- 2 teaspoons of grated ginger
- 2 tablespoons of water
- 1 seeded and chopped jalapeno
- 2 tablespoons of sugar or an alternative
- 1 large mango cut into small chunks

Instructions:
- Preheat a small saucepan over a low heat
- Place the oil, ginger, garlic and jalapeno in the pan and sauté for just around 90 seconds.
- Add the mango chunks, sugar and water.
- Turn the heat up to a medium temperature. Cover the saucepan and cook for 3 minutes, until it is boiling.
- Add the red wine vinegar and the curry powder, cook for a further minute without the lid.
- Allow to cool, stir for 5 minutes and the serve with any Indian meal.

Vegan BBQ Sauce

Ingredients:
- 1 cup of low sodium ketchup
- 3 tablespoons of barley malt syrup
- 1 teaspoon of Dijon mustard
- 3 tablespoons of water
- 2 tablespoons of extra virgin olive oil
- ½ teaspoon of garlic powder
- ¼ teaspoon of liquid smoke
- 1 ½ teaspoons of raw apple cider vinegar
- 1 teaspoon of Chile powder

Instructions:
- Simply whisk all of the ingredients together in a bowl until thoroughly mixed. Serve immediately!

Tzatziki Sauce

Ingredients:
- 1 medium sized cucumber, peeled and sliced in half.
- A pinch of cayenne pepper
- 2 cups of vegan mayonnaise
- 2 tablespoons of fresh mint
- ¼ cup of fresh lemon juice
- A pinch of ground black pepper
- 1 tablespoon of fresh dill
- 5 cloves of garlic, minced

Instructions:
- Grate the cucumber on a cheese graters' large holes.
- Combine the cucumber with the rest of the ingredients in a large bowl and mix thoroughly.
- Serve right away!

Cashew Hollandaise Sauce

Ingredients:
- 1/3 cup of soaked cashews
- 1 teaspoon of agave nectar
- 2 tablespoons of nutritional yeast
- 1 tablespoon of fresh lemon juice
- 1 teaspoon of mustard
- 1/3 cup of water
- 1/3 cup of unsweetened almond milk
- 1 tablespoon of extra virgin olive oil
- 1 teaspoon of apple cider vinegar
- A pinch of salt and pepper to taste

Instructions:
- Soak the cashew nuts for an hour in warm water.
- Drain and combine the cashews with the other ingredients in a blender.
- Blend until smooth
- Place the sauce in a saucepan and heat at a low temperature.
- Stir it with a whisk until thickened, add more water if it becomes too thick.
- Serve hot with steamed vegetables!

Conclusion

Thanks again for choosing this book, I truly hope it was able to help you begin your vegan journey. The health benefits are really quite impressive, particularly if coming from a diet rich in animal products. You will be reducing the chances of suffering from a whole myriad of diseases and conditions in the future. Not to mention doing your part in developing and protecting the rights of animals.

It's true, the vegan diet can be quite daunting to begin with. There is a lot to be aware of and for most it's a major lifestyle change. Just be sure to take it slow and ease into it. You are bound to make a couple of mistakes here and there, every vegan does! Don't get down about it, accept the mistake and keep on trucking. Over time you will find that following the principles of the diet becomes second nature.

I hope you found some inspiration in the recipes I have provided for you. Be sure to try them out and experiment over time with some additional or different flavors. People will often say that the vegan diet is boring and repetitive. This couldn't be further from the truth, all you need is a desire to experiment!

If you have enjoyed this book, then please be sure to leave a review for it!

Thanks and good luck with your vegan journey!
Jessica

Jessica Brooks

Free Ebook Offer

The Ultimate Guide To Vitamins

I'm very excited to be able to make this offer to you. This is a wonderful 10k word ebook that has been made available to you through my publisher, Valerian Press. As a health conscious person you should be well aware of the uses and health benefits of each of the vitamins that should make up our diet. This book gives you an easy to understand, scientific explanation of the vitamin followed by the recommended daily dosage. It then highlights all the important health benefits of each vitamin. A list of the best sources of each vitamin is provided and you are also given some actionable next steps for each vitamin to make sure you are utilizing the information!

As well as receiving the free ebooks you will also be sent a weekly stream of free ebooks, again from my publishing company Valerian Press. You can expect to receive at least a new, free ebook each and every week. Sometimes you might receive a massive 10 free books in a week!

All you need to do is simply type this link into your browser: http://bit.ly/18hmup4

About the Author

Hello! I'm Jessica Brooks, relatively new to the world of authorship but a veteran of the health and diet industry. If you have read any of my books, I would like to thank you from the bottom of my heart. I truly hope they have helped answer your questions and injected some inspiration into your life. Thanks to my wonderful upbringing I have been a vegetarian since infancy, making to jump to veganism nearly 20 years ago. I'm passionate about helping people improve their health! Over the coming months I am hoping to write a couple more books that will help people learn, start and succeed with certain diets.

In my spare time I am an avid reader of fantasy fiction (George Martin, you demon!). You can often find me lounging in my hammock with my latest book well into the evening. Outside of reading, I love all things physical. From hiking to sailing, swimming to skiing I'm a fan of it all! I try to practice Yoga a couple of times a week, I really recommend everyone gives it a try. You will just feel amazing after a good session!

You can find a facebook page I help manage here:

https://www.facebook.com/CleanFoodDiet

I would like to thank my publishers Valerian Press for giving me the opportunity to create this book.

Valerian Press

At Valerian Press we have three key beliefs.

Providing outstanding value: We believe in enriching all of our customers' lives, doing everything we can to ensure the best experience.

Championing new talent: We believe in showcasing the worlds emerging talent by giving them the platform to grow.

Simplicity and efficiency: We understand how valuable your time is. Our products are stream-lined and consist only of what you want. You will find no fluff with us.

We hope you have enjoyed reading Jessica's guide to the vegan diet.

We would love to offer you a regular supply of our free and discounted books. We cover a huge range of non-fiction genres; diet and cookbooks, health and fitness, alternative and holistic medicine, spirituality and plenty more. All you need to do is simply type this link into your web browser:
 http://bit.ly/18hmup4

Free Preview of "Vegan Slow Cooker Cookbook: 100 Delicious Recipes"

Tempeh chili with Vaquero beans

It's a protein packed dish for a healthy meal. Serve it over rice or quinoa for a hearty lunch or dinner.

Serves: 6

Ingredients:

- Olive oil – 2 tablespoons
- Onion – ½ small, minced
- Garlic – 3 cloves, minced
- Soy tempeh – 8 ounces, diced
- Cooked Vaquero beans – 6 cups or Pinto beans – 3 cans, rinsed and drained
- Water – 4 cups
- Tomatoes – 1 can, diced
- Tomato paste – 1 tablespoon
- Chili powder – 1 teaspoon
- Pasilla chili powder – 1 teaspoon
- Oregano – 1 teaspoon
- Paprika – 1 /2 teaspoon
- Chipotle powder – ¼-1/2 teaspoon
- Plain or smoked salt, to taste
- Cashew cream or vegan sour cream, for serving

Method

In a pan, heat olive oil and sauté onion until tender and translucent. Then add garlic and again stir fry for a few minutes. Remove from the pan. With all the other ingredients except sour cream, put onion-garlic in a slow cooker. Turn on the cooker on high and cook for 4-5 hours.

While serving, top it up with a little sour cream and enjoy!

Vegan Slow cooker Cincinnati Chili

It's a great spaghetti topping for a wholesome meal. Enjoy it either in lunch or at dinner or amuse your guests with its amazing flavors!

Note: Prepare the chili a day before if you want to devour it for lunch.

Serves: 2

Ingredients:

For morning

- Dry black beluga lentils – ¾ cup (use any other lentil if you do not want dark color chili)
- Water – 1 ½ cups
- Garlic – 2 cloves, minced
- Bay leaf – 1
- Grounded vegan crumbles – ½ cup (if you want a soy free version, then use cooked quinoa – ½ cup)
- Ground cumin – 1/2 teaspoon
- Ground hot pepper (any) – ¼ teaspoon
- Ground cinnamon – 1/8 teaspoon
- Chili powder – 1 teaspoon
- Cocoa powder – 1 teaspoon
- Ground allspice – 1 pinch

For evening

- Tomatoes – 1 ½ cups, diced
- Fresh ground nutmeg – a dash
- Salt, to taste
- Cooked pasta – 2-3 cups (for serving)

Method

In the morning, add all the morning ingredients in a 1 ½- 2 quart slow cooker and cook on low for 7-9 hours.

Half an hour before serving, open the cooker and add tomatoes, salt and nutmeg. Cook on high until the tomatoes get smashed and mixed with other ingredients.

Serve hot over cooked pasta and top it up with chopped onions or shredded vegan cheese or cooked beans, all optional though.

Grains and beans slow cooker chili

Chili can never go wrong as a main dish. It works well if you are in a mood to have a family get together or are planning for a formal event. Top it over cooked rice or pasta or simply eat with a taco or quesadillas, you'll love it all the time!

Serves: 3-4

Ingredients:

- Assorted dry beans (no kidney beans) – 2 cups
- Water – 6 cups
- Tomato puree or diced tomatoes – 1 can
- Millet – 1/8 cup
- Dry vegan bouillon – 1 tablespoon
- Cumin – 1 teaspoon
- Chili spice mix – 1 teaspoon
- Ancho powder or chipotle – ½ teaspoon
- Smoked paprika – ½ teaspoon
- Salt, to taste

Method

In a 1-1 ½ quart slow cooker, add beans and 4 cups water at night. Cook for 7-9 hours or overnight on low temperature.

In the morning, remove the beans from the cooker and rinse them. Again add beans with all other ingredients and 2 cups water. Add salt before serving. Now let everything cook on low for 7-10 hours.

Crockpot vegan bean chili with steel-cut oats

Chili is for all seasons and this one is a perfect main dish to be served over cooked quinoa or rice.

Series: 6

Ingredients:

- Water – 6 cups
- Veggie bouillon – 2 cubes
- Steel-cut oats – 1 /2 cup
- Oregano – 1 tablespoon
- Ground cumin – 2 teaspoons
- Chili powder – 1 teaspoon
- Garlic – 3 cloves, minced
- Kidney beans – 1-14.5 ounces can, drained and rinsed
- Black beans - 1-14.5 ounces can, drained and rinsed
- Tomatoes - 1-14.5 ounces can, diced
- Fire-roasted or regular frozen corns – 1 cup
- Liquid smoke, to taste
- ½ lime juice
- Salt and pepper, to taste

Method

In a 1-1 ½ quart slow cooker, add everything except lime juice and salt & pepper.

Cook for 7-10 hours on low heat. Before serving, add salt & pepper and squeeze ½ lime over chili.

To grab this exciting vegan/vegetarian cookbook be sure to search for Jessica Brooks in the amazon book/kindle store!